proclamation

Interpreting the Lessons of the Church Year

Richard L. Eslinger

6

PENTECOST 2

PROCLAMATION 6 | SERIES B

FORTRESS PRESS | MINNEAPOLIS

PROCLAMATION 6
Interpreting the Lessons of the Church Year
Series B, Pentecost 2

Scripture quotations, unless otherwise indicated, are from the New Revised Standard Version Bible, copyright © 1989 by the Division of Christian Education of the National Council of Churches in the U.S.A. and are used by permission.

Cover design: Ellen Maly
Text design: David Lott

The Library of Congress has cataloged the first four volumes of Series A as follows:

Proclamation 6, Series A: interpreting the lessons of the church
   year.
        p.   cm.
      Contents: [1] Advent/Christmas / J. Christiaan Beker — [2]
Epiphany / Susan K. Hedahl — [3] Lent / Peter J. Gomes — [4] Holy
Week / Robin Scroggs.
      ISBN 0-8006-4207-4 (v. 1 : alk. paper) — ISBN 0-8006-4208-2 (v.
2 : alk. paper) — ISBN 0-8006-4209-0 (v. 3 : alk. paper) — ISBN 0-8006-4210-4
(v. 4 : alk. paper).
      1. Bible—Homiletical use. 2. Bible—liturgical lessons,
English.
BS534.5P74   1995
251—dc20   95-4622
                                                                  CIP
        Series B:
        Advent/Christmas / Arthur Dewey—ISBN 0-8006-4215-5
        Epiphany / Mark Allan Powell—ISBN 0-8006-4216-3
        Lent / James H. Harris, Miles James Jerome, and Jerome C. Ross—
                ISBN 0-8006-4217-1
        Holy Week / Philip H. Pfatteicher—ISBN 0-8006-4218-X
        Easter / Beverly R. Gaventa—ISBN 0-8006-4219-8
        Pentecost 1 / Ched Myers—ISBN 0-8006-4220-1
        Pentecost 2 / Richard L. Eslinger—ISBN 0-8006-4221-X
        Pentecost 3 / Laura Lagerquist-Gottwald and Norman K. Gottwald—
                ISBN 0-8006-4222-8

The paper used in this publication meets the minimum requirements of American National Standard for Information Sciences—Permanence of Paper for Printed Library Materials, ANSI Z329.48-1948.

Manufactured in the U. S. A.   AF 1-4221

00   99   98   97   96   1   2   3   4   5   6   7   8   9   10

Contents

Introduction

The biblical texts for these ten Sundays after Pentecost are a rich feast of the Word. It is in Year B that the sequential readings from Mark are interrupted with a series of lections representing the entire sixth chapter of John. Our ten Sundays begin with this attention to the Fourth Gospel and then, upon completing the Bread of Life discourse, the Gospel lessons revert back to Mark. The epistle lessons derive first from Ephesians and later deal with James. The lessons from the Hebrew Scriptures are taken from the Revised Common Lectionary for two reasons. First, most every communion using the three-year lectionary either have adopted the Revised Common Lectionary or allow it as an alternative to other readings. Our attention, then, to these "Common" Old Testament lections provides the widest coverage with reference to first lessons that will actually be read and, possibly, preached. The second reason for this attention to the first lessons of the Revised Common Lectionary is their content: several absolutely central readings from the narratives of kings David and Solomon, a healthy portion of wisdom literature (the Book of Proverbs), and a taste of the Song of Solomon and the story of Esther. Rich fare indeed!

Within this rich feast of the Word for these ten Sundays, then, we preachers and our congregations are given a remarkably diverse menu of the literary forms of Scripture. Biblical narrative is present in abundance in the narratives of 2 Samuel and 1 Kings along with the readings from the Gospel of Mark. The material in John 6 begins with his treatment of the "sign" of the multiplication of the loaves and fish along with the sea crossing, both thick with narrative detail. (We should not be surprised to find so much use of irony within these stories; the narratives of the Hebrew Scriptures along with the Gospels of Mark and John contain the "mother lode" of irony in all of the Bible!) Following the crossing in John, however, the remainder of the chapter rapidly shifts to a discourse with the master image being that of "Bread of Life."

In the epistle lessons, we find the strong witness to the identity of Christ and his church that has many parallels with Paul's convictions in Colossians. In the course of these readings from Ephesians we also find hymnic material from the liturgy of the early church couched within the literary form of the epistle. Wisdom literature is present in these Sundays from both the Book of Proverbs and the Epistle of James. There has been a strong resurgence of interest in the wisdom tradition within Scripture during the past several decades and preachers are now provided with a considerable collection of excellent recent commentaries and essays. All in all, it is a great "season" in which to preach the Word during these particular ten Sundays after Pentecost. These are rich and evocative lections for the preacher; they are also in many cases a challenge for us as well.

Tenth Sunday after Pentecost
Seventeenth Sunday in Ordinary Time
Proper 12

Lectionary	First Lesson	Psalm	Second Lesson	Gospel
Revised Common	2 Sam. 11:1-15 or 2 Kings 4:42-44	Psalm 14 or Ps. 145:10-18	Eph. 3:14-21	John 6:1-21
Episcopal (BCP)	2 Kings 2:1-15	Psalm 114	Eph. 4:1-7, 11-16	Mark 6:45-52
Roman Catholic	2 Kings 4:42-44	Ps. 145:10-11, 15-18	Eph. 4:1-6	John 6:1-15
Lutheran (LBW)	Exod. 24:3-11	Psalm 145	Eph. 4:1-7, 11-16	John 6:1-15

FIRST LESSON: 2 SAMUEL 11:1-15

The story of David's adulterous and ultimately murderous actions in regard to Bathsheba and her husband Uriah is one of the most famous (infamous) of the Hebrew Scripture. It begins with a most wonderful introduction that soon turns ironic, about the spring of the year "when kings go out to battle." The story also begins with a succession of sendings that drive the plot and the characters. The irony emerges because this spring David sends (*shalach*) Joab, his officers, "and all Israel with him" to go and do battle against the Amonites. David the king, however, remains in Jerusalem. In this first verse, then, we are confronted with a king, David, who does not "go out" to do battle, but only sends his troops. The king is distanced from his true place, his righteous position at the head of his army. David is alienated from his "righteousness" as the story opens.

The scene that is then set can only occur because David has sent his warriors but remained behind. From the roof of his house he sees a woman bathing, a very beautiful woman. Sending someone to inquire as to her identity, David learns that she is Bathsheba, "wife of Uriah the Hittite" (v. 3). Learning her identity, David then sends (*shalach*) messengers to get her; Bathsheba obeys the king's command and "he lay with her" (v. 4). Notice that throughout this depiction of the actions of the two characters the initiative and responsibility lies with David and not Bathsheba. There is no implication of a mutually decided "affair"; the description is one of a forced meeting and laying down, of rape. Verse 4 adds two decisive pieces of information. First, the narrator explains that Bathsheba was purifying herself after her period, possibly implying that the woman was in her optimum time for conceiving. The narrator then adds simply that "she returned to her house." Implied here is that David has satisfied himself with Bathsheba and that no further role for her, sexual or otherwise, is anticipated. Here, for David, the story of "David and Bathsheba" has now come to its end.

That the story does not end at this point, but continues, is indicated by the narrator's information that "the woman conceived." Now it is Bathsheba's turn to "send" and she announces to David through her messenger a terse word, "I am pregnant" (v. 5). The message to David sets in motion a series of sendings now generated by the king. He sends a message to Joab, "Send me Uriah the Hittite," and Joab obeys and sends Uriah. Once in the presence of the king, David first engages him in some talk about the course of the battle before getting his plan in motion. He commands Uriah, "Go down to your house and wash your feet" (v. 8). The sexual implication of this "footwashing" is quite obvious—David's plan needs Uriah to now "lay down" with his wife. David's plan, however, cannot get in motion by virtue of Uriah's virtue. Rather than going down to his house (earlier it was described as Bathsheba's house) he stays at the king's house and sleeps with the guards there. The next day David inquires of Uriah as to why he did not go down to his own house; Uriah's response discloses his intent to remain in ritual purity and in devotion to his ruler and to his God. And while David is able to violate the ritual purity of Bathsheba, he cannot get Uriah to violate his own. Uriah makes an oath to David instead: "As you live, and as your soul lives, I will not do such a thing" (v. 11). "Bathsheba" may mean "daughter of oath," but Uriah now lives out his oath. Even a second night in Jerusalem and David's clumsy attempt to get Uriah so drunk that he will violate his oath and lay with his wife does not work. David's scheme is thwarted by Uriah's devotion to his king; his virtue is unsullied.

Now comes a sequence of sendings that attempt to preserve David's public honor and that result in Uriah's death. David writes a letter to Joab "and sent it by the hand of Uriah" (v. 14). The letter contains directions to Joab that, if followed, will result in Uriah's death in battle. Uriah unknowingly carries his own death warrant back to Joab. Upon arriving in front of the besieged city, Joab follows orders, sends Uriah into the thick of the fighting, and has his soldiers withdraw. Uriah is killed, not by the soldiers of the city, really, but by David. The king remains in Jerusalem this spring while Uriah goes off to war and to his death.

SECOND LESSON: EPHESIANS 4:1-7, 11-16

The opening three chapters of the epistle have dealt with doxology and thanksgiving, with the matters of Christian praise. Now, the author announces the subsequent content of the letter with its theme, *parakalō* ("I admonish"). The extent of this material is remarkable, spanning almost to the end of the epistle itself. At the outset, however, the *paraclesis* deals directly with the unity of the community in Christ, its character, its foundation, and its goal. Baptismal allusions abound in this opening pericope, especially in the reference to "one Body and one Spirit" (v. 4) and "one Lord, one faith, one baptism" (v. 5). Some commentators suggest that the author is quoting texts from the baptismal practice of the church while others propose baptismal catechesis as the source of these well-formed phrases. In either rendering, the baptismal ground of unity-in-Christ is being centrally affirmed here. That is the foundation not only of this initial admonition regarding unity but of these entire three chapters.

As the means to this unity, this "bond of peace" (4:3), the author sets forth three virtues as essential: humility, gentleness, and patience. (Compare this list to the five virtues St. Paul offers in Col. 3:12). Humility is also the subject of the "epiphatic" hymn to Christ in Phil. 2:1-11 and is a carefully woven thread in Luke's telling of the birth of the messiah. And again within the context of baptismal theology and practice, humility is urged of the faithful in 1 Peter 5:5. Gentleness appears as one of the markarisms in the Beatitudes (Matt. 5:5) and is commended in other epistles, particularly in response to opponents and persecutors. Patience is urged both reflecting the immeasurable divine patience that is a persistent theme throughout Scripture and underscoring the waiting of God's people for the parousia. There is, therefore, a hopefulness to all of these virtues and they constitute core virtues of Christian life. Notice, too, that humility, gentleness, and patience are both offered and admonished, they come as both gift and task (in German, as *gabe und aufgabe*). Those who are baptized in Christ are urged to live out these basic virtues in their life together; in their baptism, they are given the Sprit from which such virtues derive.

The pericope achieves its most extensive reach in the reference to the "one God and Father of all, . . ." (4:6) There are echoes of Colossians once more in this confession of "the fullness of God" (Col. 1:19) with its drive toward cosmology. Still, the primary focus remains with the church. It is only from the perspective of the baptized life in Christ that we know God as "Father" and acknowledge the fullness of divine grace. So just as the creation begins with a watery birth of all things (in Gen. 1:1, 2), so, too, the capacity to envision and live out the new creation in Christ begins with a watery birth. Both creations begin in humility and gentleness, and both entail unlimited patience, by the "God and Father of all" and by all God's people.

GOSPEL: JOHN 6:1-15; 6:16-21

John 6:1-15. The story of the miraculous feeding is the only miracle account shared by all four Gospels. Held in common are the basic elements that constitute the plot of the story—a crowd in a wilderness setting, a lack or need (their hunger), the meager resources of the loaves and fish, the pessimistic evaluation by the disciples, Jesus' words and actions (to the crowd and to God in prayer), and the feeding and miraculous abundance. Each of these narratives is then followed by the tradition of a sea crossing. Also, the issue of a sign (*sēmeia*) is typically raised within the context of the broader narrative context of the feeding story and, consequently, the issue of the true identity of Jesus (see, for example, Mark 8:11-21).

What distinguishes John's account is the dominance of imagery evoking the exodus, which thereby links the identity of Jesus to the role and person of Moses. These images include references to "the mountain" (6:3), the questioning as to food for the hunger of the people (Num. 11:3), and the "gathering" (*synagein*) of the bread/manna as a response to divine providence (Exod.16:16ff.). The acclamation of the crowd in 6:14 that "This is indeed the prophet who is to come into the world" must therefore mean a "prophet-like-Moses," given this exodus rendering of the story in John. Of course, in John, we have been formed by the Gospel narrative to always question whether an "earthly" perspective is at stake regarding our vision of Jesus' identity or one "from above."

As we have come to expect, John weaves a narrative containing the stories and images of the tradition and the dominant culture's conventional wisdom about that tradition. Alongside that rendition, John provides his own language that subverts the latter (the interpretation of the tradition by the dominant society) in favor of a new and transformed understanding of the ancient tradition fulfilled in Christ. So we bump into a kind of "anti-language" in this passage related to Exodus and the figure of Moses. First of all, we are confronted with the oddity that the Passover "was near" and yet the setting is in Galilee. Moreover, it is clear that the crowd is not composed of those making the pilgrimage to the temple—pilgrims bring along their own provisions! Then there is the Evangelist's peculiar usage of "Tiberias" as a further description of the Sea of Galilee. "Tiberias" powerfully evokes both Roman presence and power as well as the Jewish abhorrence of the unclean (the city was constructed by Herod atop a burial site). So these nonpilgrims who come to Jesus in hunger are most definitely among the poor of Israel (the barley loaves being the giveaway on this), but may also be counted as the unclean poor who may not even be welcome at the Passover festival's celebration of the exodus. This anti-language of Passover and exodus is crucial for our reading of the feeding in the Fourth Gospel since "what is positively affirmed about Jesus (in John) derives its *terms* from what is negated" (Norman Petersen, *The Gospel of John and the Sociology of Light* [Valley Forge, Pa.: Trinity Press, 1993], 98).

The tension between the language of exodus and Passover and the anti-language within the text serves to both call into question conventional approaches to Jesus' identity—a prophet who works signs—and transform the readers' vision both of Jesus and of themselves. Exodus renewed and transformed, according to the Fourth Gospel, is inherently eucharistic. In 6:10, the crowd is invited to "recline" as at a meal, and not just be present for a feeding. And the meal is to be served upon luxuriant grass, sign of God's people at rest in the presence of their Shepherd. In clear analogy to the Lord's Day meal of the Johannine community, Jesus "takes" the loaves and fish, gives thanks (*eucharistein*), and distributes the multiplied loaves and fish. Notice this clear divergence from the Synoptic feeding accounts. The disciples are not delegated with the distribution of this meal; just as at the upper room meal and at Emmaus, Jesus himself "distributed them to those who were seated" (6:11). Finally, there is a gathering of the abundant fragments left after the meal—the symbolic twelve baskets of the barley loaves. The Didache echoes this eucharistic imagery: "As this fragmented bread was scattered on the mountains, but gathered up and become one, so let your church be gathered up from the four corners of the earth into your kingdom."

But this is not the end of the story, at least in John. Seeing the sign Jesus had done, the crowds not only align him with Moses, but attempt by force to make him their king. Once more, the anti-language is striking: these people have kings in both Herod and, of course, in Caesar! But the sign has corrected their vision and they recognize their true king . . . or do they? John concludes the story by relating that in response to the crowd's intention, Jesus "fled back" to the mountain. (The NRSV's use of "withdrew" is especially weak in convey-ing Jesus' "flight.") So once more, the Evangelist has raised the issue of true vision in relation to Jesus and the signs of his identity and his mission. This much is now clear—the crowds will not be those who determine either Jesus' identity or the time at which that identity is revealed. They are right as to the kingship of Jesus, but in the wrong concerning their role both in determining that identity and the "hour" at which it will be disclosed.

John 6:16-21. In all of the Gospel accounts but one, a story of miraculous feeding is followed immediately by a sea crossing and a storm. Oddly, Luke omits the crossing following his narration of the feeding in 9:12-17. Mark serves the delightful irony of a storm in the boat following the second feeding story (Mark 8:11-21). Our version of the crossing in John is noted for its terse telling—only six short verses—but the elements held in common with the other Gospels remain evident. The disciples cross the "Sea" of Galilee (a dis-tinctly New Testament designation) with the inevitable "scene two" of the storm. In one version, Jesus is awakened to be present to the situation, while in the other (our pericope), he strides across the waves to meet the frightened dis-ciples in their storm-tossed boat. In the first version, Jesus rebuked the wind and the waves and also rebuked the disciples for their lack of faith. In the sec-ond version, however, Jesus speaks the words of self-disclosure, the divine name, and adds, "do not be afraid." Finally, through either a miraculous still-ing of the storm or a possibly miraculous deliverance to land (John's account) the disciples are saved from the sea and its fearful chaos.

As with the story of the miraculous feeding, it is where the Fourth Gospel diverges from the Synoptic traditions that the power of the narrative is most fully conveyed. Once again, we are struck by the diminution of the miraculous occurrence itself in the Johannine rendition. Mark highlights the sequence leading up to the miracle: the severity of the storm such that the boat was about to swamp, Jesus' words to the wind and the waves, and the description of the resulting calm (Mark 4:39b). Not so in John. Here, the sign is once more almost completely hidden. Rather, through archetypal images and oppositions, the focus remains fixed on Jesus, his identity, and his vocation. These images and oppositions begin with what was in the beginning for both the book of Genesis and John's own prologue—light and darkness. An "evening" setting opens the account, but once the disciples have rowed out onto the sea, John announces, "It was dark" (*skotia*). All of the issues raised in the prologue, therefore, are now back on the table—creation or chaos, belief or unbelief, life or death. By the end of the short account, all of these issues will be addressed.

If the primary opposition in John's sea crossing is depicted as visual (darkness or light), a second is developed within a spatial context. In Matthew and Mark, we are told where Jesus is and what he is doing when the disciples head off by themselves in the boat. He is back with the crowds dismissing them and then going off to the mountains to pray. Again, not so in John! Our attention in John's account is not on Jesus going off from the crowds and the disciples, but on the disciples' movement away from Jesus. John's announcement that "Jesus had not yet come to them" (v. 17c) both underscores this spatial separation and sets up the reader's expectation that this separation will be overcome by virtue of Jesus' own initiative. In the darkness upon a sea grown increasingly "awakened" (*diegeireto*), the disciples continue to row into the storm, ironically separating themselves even more from Jesus. Their prognosis is dire. The sudden appearance of Jesus walking on the sea fills the Twelve momentarily with fear. That fear is short-lived for two reasons. First, their Lord announces the *ego eimi*, and adds, "do not be afraid" (v. 20). Also, the boat that had been located by John as three or four miles from the shore now "immediately" reaches land. There is no longer need for fear from the storm itself nor from the appearance of the Lord, who comes to fearful followers striding on the sea.

HOMILETICAL STRATEGIES

I. Narrative Preaching. This is a Sunday for narrative preaching. Both the Gospel lesson of the miraculous feeding in John and the first lesson of David and Bathsheba are powerful stories of the biblical tradition. The best advice when dealing with such narratives is to preach a narrative sermon. There is really no need in either case, moreover, to append a nonnarrative prologue or epilogue to the narrative homiletical plot. "Running the story" (Lowry) is the preferred approach. Within each option—the preacher cannot really compress these two stories into one sermon—the challenge is to deal with setting and characterization effectively and to contemporize the story at certain opportune locations. The preacher then may put the narrative on "pause" and develop an excursus that explores "how this place is for us now." Probably, each sermon can best contain three or four of these excursi. We now can look at possible locations within each sermonic plot for such contemporizations:

The Miraculous Feeding. John tells us that the Passover was near. That event has firmly established a "family" of images in Israel's memory—wilderness, the "crowd," the mountain, and hunger. Two other images of exodus typology are missing at the story's outset, those of leading and of feeding. Both will shortly be provided. The first excursus is sparked by Jesus' question regarding provision, "Where are we going to buy bread for these people to eat?" (6:5). Philip's response is one of "realism"; from the perspective of the Fourth Gospel, he answers from an "earthly" point of view. Expand here for the congregation how "Philipism" is always poised ready to give good answers as to why a fresh Spirit-given vision for the church is impossible. Either we cannot afford it—"six months wages . . ."—or we do not have the leadership. The list goes on. As the preacher, you can come up with the other good reasons why Philipism in the church predictably rises to quash a new vision of our vocation and journey.

A second excursus relates to the provisions that the disciples do discover, a little boy with two barley loaves and five little fish. These barley cakes are the food of the poor; they are a clear sign that this child and his family are among the poorest in Israel. Yet he offers them to Jesus to be used on behalf of the need of the multitude. Usually, our stance toward the poor is that it is our task to provide for them. Here, the little boy reverses our conventional wisdom. The text of the hymn from the Hispanic Church, "Cuando El Pobre," speaks to this first miracle of the miraculous feeding:

> When the poor ones who have nothing share with strangers,
> When the thirsty water gives unto us all, . . .
> Then we know that God still goes that road with us.

The next excursus may be located when Jesus commands the disciples to "make the people sit down" (v. 10). A series of transitions are being made here, first from the identity of "crowd" to that of a "people" (recall the image of "people" within the wilderness family of images). Other transitions are soon discovered, from anxiety to peace, from frantic trekking about to being at rest, and from hunger to being fed. Most centrally, the crowd is becoming a people. Analogies within the life of the parish may well be explored here. Of course, the eucharistic action itself in v. 11 offers itself for contemporary exploration; in fact, if the sermon is preached at the eucharist, it would be somewhat odd not to develop this excursus of the analogy between the miraculous feeding and the Holy Meal. Finally, the epilogue to the story offers another possible occasion to explore "how it is for us." Jesus now commands that the fragments from the meal be gathered up "so that nothing may be lost" (v. 12) Those of us called to preach will probably want to explore for the congregation this insistence of our Lord "that nothing may be lost."

David and Bathsheba. A similar approach will work with the Old Testament narrative as well. Here, the preacher may well pause and explore that self-contradiction—David remaining at home when "kings go out to battle." Perhaps other, more contemporary contradictions within the church also come to mind. A further excursus can focus on David's attempted cover-up, begun when he commands, "Send me Uriah the Hittite." The cover-up, of course, was an attempt by David to avoid the consequences of his "sending" for Bathsheba. Now, analogies within our lived experience also come to mind ("Watergate" and all the other "Gates" that have since come to light). There is a faithfulness and loyalty demonstrated by Uriah upon his arrival back in Jerusalem which stand in strong contrast to David's character. Furthermore, Uriah is a foreigner, here living with more integrity than the great king. This irony will lead to tragedy. The preacher might spot other ironies within the community's life and the nation's life where irony leads to tragedy. Finally, Uriah's fate is sealed as he makes an oath that he then keeps (v. 11). We live in a culture where the keeping of promises is often ignored or even treated with disdain; one men's movement calls itself "Promise

Keepers." One might explore here the conditions that lead to such movements and the importance of the oath for a person of Uriah's integrity. The final irony in the pericope is that Uriah carries back with him the orders for his own death. We may need to point to the consequences that result from virtue and servanthood. They are not always glowing rewards and promotions. We often refer to these virtuous members of the church as "martyrs"!

II. Ephesians 4:1-7, 11-16. The pastoral context for preaching will probably be the guide for our homiletic use of the Ephesians text. But the text's witness to both the church's essential unity in vv. 4 and 5 as well as the celebration of diversity with regard to the gifts of the Spirit is a balance sorely needed in the church situation today. Our culture elevates "pluralism" to the highest good and many in the church go along with this latest "wind of doctrine" (4:14). This particular wind of doctrine, however, will admit of no center to diversity that claims truth for itself, no particularity that can locate diverse gifts around a center that holds. That achievement, on the other hand, is precisely the gift of the Gospel as declared in the Ephesians text.

A sermon on the pericope, then, could begin with a focus on the "pluralism" that becomes chaos in both church and society. Images here easily come to mind. (The challenge in preaching this text is that even more powerful images will need to be brought to bear in the subsequent affirmation of this unity in Christ!) Once the hearers are nicely focused on the images embodying the chaos of our "spirit of the age," a next move or single meaning can involve the affirmation of the unity that is given through our baptism into Christ. Notice that it is first of all a gift. Baptismal imagery will come into play here, especially appropriate if a baptism or baptismal renewal by the congregation occurs on this Lord's Day. This second move in the sermon will also underscore the work of the Spirit in working the unity of the one body. Still, we do keep breaking "the bond of peace" (4:3). This third move, then, may focus on the ways in which unity is fractured through those things we have done and those we have not done. While the first move in the sermon has a more "external" focus—on the world's disunity—this third move is ecclesial, its illustrations need to be derived from our life in the body.

One obvious source of imagery these days is the "great fracture" between liberals and evangelicals in most of our churches. Other sources may be tapped that are more local and parish-centered in their expressions. A final move is necessary that then admonishes us all toward that unity which first has come as a gift from God. Here, the second aspect of the Spirit's work may be developed; it is that same Spirit of unity which grants us a rich diversity of gifts to build up the body. Once more we have a single meaning that is the strongest in the sermon. Our image system here will need to match strength to strength. Notice that this is not the place to provide more examples of "what not to do." The challenge for us preachers is to invite the assembly to see and hear ways in which these gifts of the Spirit are being used or can be used to build up the Body of Christ. Again, the rule is, when imaging or illustrating, match "strength to strength."

Eleventh Sunday after Pentecost
Eighteenth Sunday in Ordinary Time
Proper 13

Lectionary	First Lesson	Psalm	Second Lesson	Gospel
Revised Common	2 Sam. 11:26—12:13a or Exod. 16:2-4, 9-15	Ps. 51:1-12 or Ps. 78:23-29	Eph. 4:1-16	John 6:24-35
Episcopal (BCP)	Exod. 16:2-4, 9-15	Ps. 78:1-25 or 78:14-20, 23-25	Eph. 4:17-25	John 6:24-35
Roman Catholic	Exod. 16:2-4, 12-15	Ps. 78:3-4, 23-25	Eph. 4:17, 20-24	John 6:24-35
Lutheran (LBW)	Exod. 16:2-15	Ps. 78:23-29	Eph. 4:17-24	John 6:24-35

FIRST LESSON: 2 SAMUEL 11:26—12:13a

The first two verses of the pericope conclude the saga of David, Bathsheba, and Uriah. Upon Uriah's death, there is an appropriate mourning by Bathsheba and, upon its completion, the situation changes with suddenness. Once more, there is a sending from David who brings Bathsheba to his house (recall "the house of Bathsheba" and "the house of Uriah" in chap. 11) where she becomes his wife and bears him a son. The succession of events is so rapid they practically fall over each other! However, the narrator adds a piece of information that has not been shared thus far in the story—"the thing that David had done displeased the Lord" (v. 27b). What had seemed to be a sequence of events arriving at a new stability for David becomes radically unstable upon the reader's learning of the displeasure of David's God.

The sendings within the story continue, but now from God's side; Nathan is sent by God to David the king. Immediately Nathan sets forth a parable, the story of the rich man and the poor man with one ewe. Because of the nature of the parable, David's role is formally to pass judgment on the evildoer and to vindicate the one who suffers injustice. In that role, as he listens to the story, he is "righteous" in his office as Israel's king. Upon hearing of the parable's conclusion, with its tragic ending for the poor man and the greed of the rich, David becomes filled with anger (*aph*). The phrase is intensified through repetition in Hebrew, translated "greatly kindled." Clearly judgment is due the utterly selfish rich man, especially, as David comments, because he had no pity (*chamal*). That judgment comes in the form of an oath (recall "Bathsheba": daughter of oath); the rich man deserves to die (v. 5b). The prophet's reply is swift and blunt. Nathan states to David, "You are the man!" The parable has done its work and there is the shock of recognition. David is the man.

While David is still speechless, Nathan continues with a prophetic oracle from the Lord. Now we finally hear a messenger directly in the continuing story. The message from the Lord recites all of the providence shown to David, and all of the blessings God has bestowed—anointing, rescuing, and givings, all lavished upon David by God. And Nathan adds for the Lord a cutting and ironic statement of this divine grace: "And if that had been too little, I would have added as much more" (v. 8). Then in his own voice, the prophet Nathan adds his own condemnation of David, commenting in detail on the deeds that were evil in God's sight. In v. 9b, the indictment forms a brief chiasm, with reference to the murder of Uriah being mentioned both before and after the naming of David's adultery with Bathsheba. The effect is to frame in David's deed with Bathsheba with his murderous deed to Uriah—murder-adultery-murder. David cannot escape. He is condemned by his own words. The particulars of the condemnation come once more in oracular form and are in counterpoint to the recital of the blessings given earlier. Now, much shall be taken away and while David's evil deeds may have been done in secret, God promises to do this deed "before all Israel, and before the sun" (v. 12). David is no longer the one who renders judgment. He is judged by God and admits to his guilt. Now the words echo back to David and to the reader, "deserves to die." However, the sin of the king is "put away," but not without consequences both immediate and far-reaching (see vv. 15b-25). But as for David, there is grace once more; the oracle's final word of the Lord is that in spite of deserving to die, David shall live.

SECOND LESSON: EPHESIANS 4:17-25

Once more, there is an admonition to the Ephesians, this time underlined by the opening direct address: "I affirm and insist on in the Lord." Even if not written by Paul, the author of Ephesians takes on the mantle of apostolic authority, and in a very Pauline manner. What follows is a binary system related to life in the world and life within the new community in Christ. How to speak of those who remain separated from God in Christ is a translator's challenge. The NRSV gives us "Gentiles" for "*ta ethne*," but earlier references in 2:11 and 3:1 are clearly meant to refer to Gentile Christians. "Pagans" may be too strong here, but the description of these "people" is in stark contrast to those sharing new life with Christ. The binary contrast between those "people" and God's people involves both the inmost character of one's being along with the public actions which issue from that inner condition. In the case of those "people," the core issues are ignorance (*agnoia*) and hardness of heart that leave them both alienated from God and devoted to a variety of Godless actions. The former, ignorance, can be viewed either as deriving from separation from God or as a cause of that separation. Certainly the two are related. However, this *agnoia*, this ignorance, is not intended to refer to simply a benign lack of certainties regarding theology. This ignorance is an active rejection of the knowledge of God, a "darkened understanding," and its consequences are deadly. Alongside this assertive ignorance is "hardness of heart," a favorite expression in the narratives of the Hebrew Scriptures and the Gospels for characters whose actions oppose the divine will. Both terms, "ignorance" and "hardness of heart," connote a willful turning away from God; these are not just plain and simple folks who do not yet have the right information on which to build their lives!

In v. 19, the writer offers a short list of the ethical consequences of this inward condition and its alienation from God. We note first that most Pauline listings of these vices are both more extensive and more concrete in their reference. Here, however, the "practices" are only alluded to while the condition driving the symptoms is highlighted. There is an insatiable quality to the passions of those who are alienated from God. While excesses of sexuality are certainly implied in this listing, the greed should be construed as affecting all of human life, a covetousness that cannot remedy itself. That remedy can only come from being removed from the darkness and dwelling in the light.

The binary opposite is strongly contrasted: "not so . . . you" who "learned Christ" (v. 20). Notice, though, that the writer of the epistle does not immediately provide the structural alternates to the inner condition and outward manifestations of those who are alienated from God. Rather, there is a reminder of the preaching by which the hearers first heard of Christ and the catechesis through which they were formed in his image. Those who "learned Christ" did so by hearing the truth as they were being taught it. This latter side of the binary equation, then, reintroduces the baptismal motif encountered in the previous week's lection. In both its structure and its rhetoric, this rehearsal of our baptismal identity follows upon Col. 3:8-9. There is an "old self"/"new self" dichotomy with references to what has been laid aside and what has been heard and received. The image of being clothed is a particularly central baptismal reference and quite naturally is located following the mention of what is renounced. (Many of the reformed baptismal liturgies in the churches today now follow this ancient sequence of renunciation, affirmation of faith in Christ, and, following baptism, being "clothed" in white.)

Now, in vv. 24 and 25, the writer portrays the new life of those who have been taught Christ. These who are God's people, who are "renewed in the spirit of your minds," have an inner condition of holiness and true righteousness. That inner state, however, is constantly being renewed—the believer has as active a role in maintaining these inner qualities as the "Gentiles" have in maintaining their state of ignorance and hardness of heart. But those who have learned Christ, and are clothed with him, are now admonished to live out the gift that has been given. We will "see" what these people have heard by how they live together as "members of one another" and we will "hear" what they have learned as they preach and teach in our midst (v. 25).

GOSPEL: JOHN 6:24-35

With the crowds finding the object of their search—Jesus—the narrative following the sea crossing now recovers and even intensifies the exodus motif. At the outset, however, the question from the crowd both injects a dissonance into the story and invites the reader to decide on the true answer. Jesus had left the crowd, we recall, at the mount of multiplication when they had already announced him a "prophet" and were about to make him their king. Their opening address of "Rabbi," therefore, seems to signal a forgetfulness of any earlier insights into Jesus' identity. The question itself is difficult since it asks a "when" and "where" simultaneously—"when did you come to be here?" (the verb "to be" is omitted in the NRSV). Once more, the reader is to decide between earthly meanings and those "from above." Is the crowd just checking into Jesus' schedule and itinerary or are they unknowingly and ironically asking from whom Jesus comes? Jesus deals with the earthly issue first. The crowd is seeking him out because they got their bellies full of bread before. He underlines their disinterest in things from above; their quest was "not because you saw signs" (v. 26).

Jesus' next statement is definitely about those things from above, and includes such recurring Johannine themes as faithful "work" and things that "abide" as well as his distinctive notion of eternal life. All of these are now located in relation to the image of food (about to become reframed as "bread") just as they were aligned with water in the Woman at the Well narrative in chap. 4. This food that abides for eternal life will be given by the Son of Humanity and not provided on a periodic basis by a handy rabbi! As if to underscore the worlds of difference between the two points of view, Jesus utters those enigmatic words about the One upon whom "the Father has set his seal" (v. 27). Various commentators have interpreted this act of sealing as referring to Jesus' baptism, his being lifted up upon a cross and to glory, or to the entirety of the incarnation as announced in the prologue. However it is to be construed, perhaps even that enigmatic quality itself, the statement evokes a further question from the crowd that now propels the discourse more forcefully in the direction of the exodus event. The crowd wants Jesus to tell them what to do to "work the works of God." "Believe," Jesus answers, believe in him whom God has sent.

In the other Gospels, the question might have led to a Sermon on the Mount or perhaps a series of parables of the kingdom. But instead, the Fourth Evangelist gives us a reenactment of the exodus in miniature with the role of the crowd being played by the crowd. The question is, What role will Jesus play? Once more the crowd (played by the crowd) asks for a sign that has already been given. And once more, at the discourse level, the readers of the story are invited to spot the misunderstanding and forgetfulness, notice the connections to their Scriptures, and more deeply understand the work of believing in this One who is sent. Apparently, we conclude, the crowd will only extend the work of faith in the face of signs but will still not get it right. They do recall to Jesus that their ancestors ate manna in the wilderness, that God "gave them bread from heaven to eat" (v. 31). The invitation between the lines is for Jesus to take the role of Moses and give them manna once more. (By the first century in rabbinic thought, the manna had become associated with the gift of God's Word and wisdom. Clearly in our story, however, the crowd searches only for bread.)

HOMILETICAL STRATEGIES

2 Samuel 11:26-12-13. The story of Nathan and David is one of consequences to actions, consequences that ultimately cannot be avoided because they are of God. The pericope begins with a portrayal of a newly achieved domesticity. David finally has Bathsheba and also has a new son. The situation looks bright and stable. However, the narrator informs us that "the thing that David had done displeased the LORD" (11:27). All of a sudden, we look for the consequences of that divine displeasure; stability has been overturned. The appearance of Nathan, sent by God, brings with him the parable of the rich man and the poor man. Upon hearing of the greed and unrighteousness of the rich man, the king's response is to impose consequences—"the man . . . deserves to die." This sentence sets up the dramatic moment of reversal; the prophet announces, "You are the man!" Now we are sure that David's sin will bear consequences, perhaps including the loss of the king's own life. The covenant recital in which Nathan speaks for God also deals in consequences, in this case consequences thwarted by David's actions. All of the rising fortune of David, we learn, had come from God and if that had not been enough, God "would have added that much more" (v. 8). The implied consequences of such grace should have been seen in David's righteous deeds as king of Israel. Indeed, we should have been able to see in David's life the gratitude to God for all that David had received. Instead, the covenant is broken and God's grace is treated as a privilege to be abused. The consequences of breaking covenant are now spelled out in ironic detail. David kills Uriah by the sword, now David's house shall know the sword all his days. David has taken Uriah's wife for his own in secret; now David's own wives will be taken by others publicly, "in the sight of this very sun" (12:12). But grace is reasserted and covenant is reestablished with the king chosen by God—David shall not die. Clearly this consequence is all grace. In David's own words, he deserves to die. The prophet announces that grace—the word of the Lord is that "you shall not die" (12:13).

The preacher may want to take each of these consequences in succession and treat them from within the story. Certainly contemporary analogies exist to each and may be briefly mentioned. (We do not want to elaborate a large story-illustration in the sermon; the entire story with its parable will want to remain dominant.) What we may also want to do is to develop a section of the sermon that speaks of our own actions and their consequences. The subjects here should be carefully defined. We may point to behaviors in the "world out there" that are having unavoidable consequences. In fact, one of the myths of our liberal culture is that actions should not need to have consequences! But the preacher will also remind the congregation that at the heart of the matter here is covenant and therefore the issue of God's own people and their right-eousness. We will need to point to these deeds with such Nathan-like effec-tiveness that all of us may hear the word of judgment, "You are the person!" That word, of course, sets up the possibility of repentance and restitution. It also sets up the possibility of hearing a new word of grace, which the preacher will certainly want to speak as well.

Ephesians 4:17-25. The preacher here is preaching to the baptized. Not mere-ly that; the preacher is inviting those baptized in Christ to remember who they are and also become more alert as to who they are not. Apart from the issue of authorship, we have a very Pauline kind of dialectic operating in the text at the theological level. That dialectic is embodied in the baptismal liturgy and may become the basis for the movement and direction of the sermon. The ancient and reformed baptismal liturgies begin with the *renuncio*, with the insistence that the candidates renounce the world in its sin and its darkness.

Our sermon could begin, then, with an invitation to recall the most recent baptism within the parish or to anticipate one that will be celebrated later on this day (this is an obvious Sunday for Holy Baptism or the congregational renewal of their baptismal vows!). The focus in this first section of the sermon is on the *renuncio*, on what we have all turned away from in our baptisms. Whatever the particular ethical practices we may point toward in the sermon— which are dependent on the pastoral situation and the context for ministry— the pericope invites us all to probe more deeply. Underlying any and all sinful deeds is the "big, fat, relentless ego." Its greed is insatiable, its ignorance is willful, and its compassion has grown sclerotic. Now the preacher must image this condition. The challenge here is not a poverty of illustration but a homilet-ical discipline that keeps the examples terse and well-focused. To keep integri-ty with the text, shape the image-system here in such a way that more than just the individual expression of evil is portrayed. The evil that a Christian must renounce is both profoundly personal and intensely social in its dimensions and its consequences.

Now comes the other side of the dialectic. In the baptismal liturgy the drama now moves to adhesion to Christ, to public affirmation of faith in the Triune God, and to the baptismal death and rising with Christ. There is a ritual expression of this being clothed with a new self as the new babes in Christ come up out of the waters. Immediately they are clothed with a white robe symbolizing this new self. Once more, the focus is both on those specific deeds that reflect this new being in Christ and on the underlying new humanity of the believer. A danger in this sermon is that the expressions of evil given example in the prior section will be more concretely imaged than expressions of the holiness of those living out their baptism in Christ. And it is even more critical that the examples of this holiness of Christian life be seen in both its personal and communal dimensions. The pericope concludes precisely on that note: "We are members of one another" (4:25).

John 6:24-35. The pericope is a challenge to preachers, primarily because its opening sequence continues the sign narrative of the Miraculous Feeding. The latter portions of the text, however, shift to become a discourse leading up to the *ego eimi* proclamation about "bread of life." As in the other Johannine discourses, there is a dialogue between Jesus and another character in this case, "the crowd" and the dialogue eventually evolves into a soliloquy by Jesus addressed to the reader. The narrative plot related to the sign disappears in the process. We will not want to revert back to the old method of extracting some thematic from the passage and thereby leaving behind its mobility, its structure, and its intention. Rather, we may shape a sermonic plot comprised of several "moves" or single meanings designed to both form and perform in the hearing of the congregation. Each of these locations of single meaning will then need to be imaged out of the lived experience of the hearers. The sequence of moves may be designed as follows:

"Look at the crowd out there on the Sea. There is a flotilla of need coming across the lake."

(Image this cargo of need with reference to both some general human cargo—anxiety, sickness and hunger—as well as some specific needs from the life of the community of faith and drawn from the world.)

"They look for Jesus, come to him, hoping to get just enough help to get by for another day."

(There is a song, "Help Me Make It Through the Night." The crowds come to Jesus to ask him to help them make it through the day. Of course, they do not know who Jesus really is or what he is really offering.)

"Jesus announces the end of their hunger. 'Bread of life,' he offers. 'I am the bread come down from heaven.'"

(The rule is to match positive images with positive conceptual meanings. We will not give further images of need here, but of feeding. Obviously the eucharist is the church's central image of this "bread of heaven." What other images relate to the bread of life [food pantry, a wedding banquet, homemade bread offered to a newcomer/visitor, dinner on the grounds at a church homecoming] within the community?)

"But how can we get this bread?" we ask. Jesus answers, "Believe in the One who is sent, in the Bread from Heaven."

(The meaning to be imaged or illustrated is that of true belief, of belief in Jesus as the Bread of life. Our "work" is both to share bread with the hungry and to believe in God's Son. Probably a story illustration is best here. What individual, or better, what community, shows forth this care for the hungry along with this belief in the Bread Come Down from Heaven?)

Twelfth Sunday after Pentecost
Nineteenth Sunday in Ordinary Time
Proper 14

Lectionary	First Lesson	Psalm	Second Lesson	Gospel
Revised Common	2 Sam. 18:5-9, 15, 31-33 or 1 Kings 19:4-8	Psalm 130 or Ps. 34:1-8	Eph. 4:25—5:2	John 6:35, 41-51
Episcopal (BCP)	Deut. 8:1-10	Psalm 34 or 34:1-8	Eph. 4:(25-29) 30 —5:2	John 6:37-51
Roman Catholic	1 Kings 19:4-8	Ps. 34:2-9	Eph. 4:30—5:2	John 6:41-51
Lutheran (LBW)	1 Kings 19:4-8	Ps. 34:1-8	Eph. 4:30—5:2	John 6:41-51

FIRST LESSON: 2 SAMUEL 18:5-9, 15, 31-33

The lection picks up the story of the rebellion of Absalom in midstride and omits the dramatic scene of the messengers running to tell David of the "good news" of the battle. At the outset of the lection, some key information is given regarding the climax of the conflict between Absalom and his father (the name "Absalom" means "my Father is peace"!). David divides his private army of professionals into three groups and in the hearing of all orders his commanders to "Deal gently for my sake with the young man Absalom" (v. 5). The battle takes place in a forest, fought by David's mercenaries against the perhaps much less experienced "men of Israel." Even though outnumbered, David's forces secure complete victory, scattering and killing Absalom's force. At the end, the narrator leaves the reader with only one opponent of David still alive there in the forest of Ephraim—the king's rebellious son Absalom. He has caught his head in the branches of a tree while riding his mule and "was left hanging between heaven and earth" (v. 9). (Notice that the text does not have Absalom hanging by his hair. That tradition is an embellishment by Josephus and the Talmud.) The question either way, however, is how gently David's generals will deal with Absalom, hanging there between heaven and earth.

The lection now skips to the death of Absalom at the hands of "ten young men" who are Joab's armor-bearers. What is omitted is the crucial interplay between Joab and one of his men in which Joab clearly seeks to have Absalom killed, even to the point of an implied bribe (v. 12). Nevertheless, the soldier heeds his king's desires for Absalom's safety; it is up to Joab, his cousin, to do the deed. That the ten young men are noted by the narrator as the ones who do the killing, the omitted information is significant. Absalom dies up there between heaven and earth at the hand of cousin Joab. Now all that is needful is to give Absalom a decent burial, which he does not receive at Joab's hand, and to report the events to King David. The puzzling depiction of two messengers running to tell David the news is variously explained by interpreters as either the conflation of two separate traditions of the story or as the consequence of Joab's attempts to manipulate the way in which David hears the "tidings." From the perspective of the situation at the end of their journey back to David, however, the arrival of two figures allows for the suspense to be extended and for David to hear those tidings as a succession of messages. The narrator first shifts point of view back to that of the king, "sitting between two gates" (v. 24). One figure appears, running alone. In response to the sentinel, David comments that there must be news. The appearance of a second runner increases David's certainty—"He also is bringing tidings" (v. 26). When the first runner arrives and announces "All is well!" he falls at David's feet and praises God for the victory. In response to David's question about the well-being of Absalom, the first messenger, Ahimaaz becomes vague, speaking only of the "great tumult" (v. 29). Then David turns to the second messenger and asks again concerning Absalom. The Cushite is more direct in his tidings; there is "good tidings." Of course the tidings are good to everyone loyal to David except to David himself. Deeply moved, David retires to his chamber and grieves. The lament is among the most poignant in Scripture. Within one breath, David speaks "my son" five times and names Absalom twice. The repetition drives home the mourning of David the king. Only by this "victory could he remain king, yet its taste is bitter indeed: "Would I had died instead of you," David cries out to his dead son. Absalom's father will know peace no more.

SECOND LESSON: EPHESIANS 4:25—5:2

Following the development of the "old" and "new" person in Christ motif in the previous pericope, the epistle now becomes more concrete regarding these alternatives. The initial section of this turn to praxis identifies four conditions that represent the old life before Christ—speaking lies, being angry, stealing, and spreading evil (or "idle") talk. The list is not meant to be an exhaustive list of vices nor does it particularly establish internal relationships between them. They are selected for mention, perhaps, because of the pastoral situation at Ephesus. Indeed, if they do not represent some of the central oppositions to the new life of the body, why bring them up in the first place? Having been brought up, however, the author then elaborates on each, though with differing interests in each regard. In the course of these elaborations, the issues at hand are connected to other motifs within the epistle as well.

In the case of speaking falsehood rather than the truth (4:25), the expanded comment provides the reason for truthtelling—"we are all members of one another." The metaphor of the body surfaces with much the same sequence from theological claim to ethical imperative as seen in 1 Cor. 12:12-27. This dynamic also presents the reader once again with a shift from an initial concern for the individual—speaking no lies—to a focus on the communal context for new life in Christ. Just as truth proceeds from God, so too, in Christ, it is to proceed from the believer-in-community. Here, we are given a prolepsis of the latter admonition to be "imitators of God" (5:1). By contrast, the vice of anger is not elaborated with reference to its binary virtue within the new life. Rather, by way of proverbial wisdom, the caution against anger is reinforced. The sun is not to set on our anger (or wrath) and we are not to make room for the devil by holding on to anger. (Here, the devil is *diabolos*, the personification of all opposition to God rather than "Satan" the divine prosecutor. The latter is more typical of Pauline usage while Ephesians and the catholic epistles typically construe the devil as the tempter, *diabolos*.)

The text shifts again as the third vice, stealing, is highlighted. Here, the discussion remains on the ethical level, with the admonition being contrasted with the practical consequences of abandoning the vice and living fully within the new life in Christ. By leaving behind any acts of theft, the believer is presented with the opportunity to give more fully and freely to those in need. The opposition is surprisingly not between stealing and not stealing, but between theft and acts of compassion. Subtly, the question of the inner and outer conditions of the new and the old humanity are expanded here. New life in Christ does not remain satisfied with only a putting away of evil (theft), but of the good that springs from the believers' being clothed with holiness. Finally, the attention of the readers is turned to a repudiation of evil, or idle speech. Once again there is an echo of the body metaphor through the construction image we saw used in 4:12 (*oikodomēn*, to "build up"). And once again, the image of baptism is introduced by way of the reference to the "seal for the day of redemption" (4:30). This reference to "the day" conveys the eschatological dimension of baptism in Christ and, as we would expect, the work of the Spirit is mentioned in this baptismal context. The particular admonition not to grieve the Holy Spirit, however, is distinctive and allusive. Other biblical references included Isa. 63:12 and, possibly, 1 Thess 4.8. On the basis of some meager later allusions, there is a faint possibility that the phrase represents the church's memory of a Jesus saying whose context is otherwise lost.

The pericope ends by expanding the field of view from specific ethical admonitions to a vision of the holiness of God: "be imitators of God," encourages the writer. One use of this *analogia relationis* (Karl Barth) is contained in Luke's Sermon on the Plain: "Be merciful, just as your Father is merciful." To continue with Barth's schema, it is not that Christians are to be analogies to the Divine Being, *anologia entis*, but are to be "analogies of relationship." The writer of Ephesians has now provided four specific alternatives whereby we can deny that relationship or reflect it into the world's darkness. Or to shift the imagery, we can reject that relationship and continue to act ike the rest of the odoriferous world, or become, to the world's surprise, a fragrant offering to Christ.

GOSPEL: JOHN 6:37-51

Twice before, Jesus has announced himself as *egō eimi*, as the divine "I am," first to the Samaritan woman and then to the wave-swept disciples. Now, the

Evangelist begins a series of "I am" statements by Jesus that add some profound and striking imagery to the communal imagination of the covenant people. To the crowds at the synagogue at Capernaum, near the time of the Passover, comes the first of these images—"bread of life." In the history of interpretation, this image is typically located within either the orbit of Israel's wisdom tradition or the church's eucharistic theology and practice. In the former case, the allusions are to the ways and means of God's revelation that become bread to the wise. So, to respond positively to Jesus as "bread of life" is, for John, to believe in his word, to abide in the word, and to thereby have life. The second, eucharistic, connotation of the image serves several functions: It links the immediately prior sign of the multiplication of the loaves with the upper room meal, it links the eucharist to God's provision of manna to Israel in the wilderness, and it connects the eucharist to a powerful sense of the real presence of the Lord. Perhaps these alternative interpretations do not present us with an either-or necessity; the text may travel as an ellipse around both the sapiential and eucharistic models of interpretation.

That the discourse occurs as "the Passover, the festival of the Jews, was near" (6:4) aligns it with the two dominant narratives of the synagogue readings for the observance: the exodus and the creation accounts. In fact, some have suggested that the discourse as a whole represents a rabbinical-style homily on these Passover texts, a possibility enhanced by the synagogue location itself. The exodus theme permeates the bread of life discourse. Jesus now "come(s) down from heaven" (v. 38) as did the manna in the wilderness. The distinction, though, is crucial here and is a life-or-death matter (see vv. 47-51). Also echoing the exodus narrative is the motif of rebellion, the murmuring and complaining of the people (vv. 41, 43). Jesus is portrayed as a lawgiver like Moses, but much more. He is the new manna which is living bread, that is, bread which brings life. The creation account provides additional insights into the discourse. The disobedient couple are driven out of the garden by their Creator, but now Jesus announces that "anyone who comes to me I will never drive away" (v. 37). Moreover, the advent of death as a consequence of the actions of Adam and Eve is now contraindicated by the Father's new act of sending the Son. To eat this bread come down from heaven is to live forever (vv. 50-51).

The oppositions within the narrative, therefore, derive from these points of view on the primary image of Jesus as bread of life. And the oppositions are what drives the discourse on to its finale in v. 51. Above all else, the discourse insists, death and life are at stake in this *egō eimi* self-revelation by Jesus; the opposition is tied as well to those of unbelief and belief. Two other oppositions add to the tension within the discourse beyond those of life–death and belief–unbelief. The first opposition is that of becoming a believer in Jesus or remaining one of "the Jews." Since this term, "the Jews," most recently has had as its reference the Judeans who are in opposition to Jesus, it is surprising in 6:41 to hear this Galilean crowd in the Capernaum synagogue described in this manner. Notice, however, that the designation comes only after the crowd joins with their ancestors in murmuring about bread come down from heaven. This murmuring continues as the people ironically question Jesus' origins in spite of the *egō eimi* disclosure—"the son of Joseph, whose father and mother we know" (v. 42a). Apparently, the chosen people can become lumped with "the Judeans" no matter where they reside if there is only disbelief and complaint in the face of divine self-revelation and bread from heaven! The issue of the identity of those who are chosen provides the second of these oppositions. How to explain the unbelief of God's own people to the gift of God's own Word made flesh is an issue that was stated as early as the prologue to the Gospel (1:11, 12) Now, we hear Jesus announce that he will never "drive away" anyone who comes to him and will not lose anything given him by the Father. Yet disbelief and murmuring remain. Ironic is the only way to describe the mystery that some of God's own people refuse to be drawn to their God and to the One who has been sent to them. The positive side of the same equation is given at the end of the pericope in v. 51. Those who do eat this bread will live forever. And the magnitude of the "draw" is underscored by a shift in terms. The bread from heaven is given for the life of "the world" (*tou kosmou*).

HOMILETICAL STRATEGIES

John 6:37-51. The narrative material at the beginning of John 6 has faded away almost entirely by the time we reach the Gospel lesson for this Sunday. Only one interjection from the crowd retains the element of a conversation within the text—the complaint in v. 42. Instead, a discourse by the Lord is addressed "over the heads" of the crowd directly to the church. And here, the only element of conversation from our side may be that of complaint as well! Due to the strong presence of exodus imagery, our homiletical strategy may begin by locating the congregation in the wilderness. After all, that is where we hunger and thirst and where Jesus addresses these words to us about the bread from heaven. A sermon may then be plotted representing Jesus' conversation with us.

1. Jesus addresses a wilderness people. Out here, there is constant need and daily threat, both of which are rather out of our control. This wilderness location may be first disclosed when we or loved ones become seriously ill or when there is a profound loss. For others, it is revealed when they encounter rejection and indifference at the hands of others. And at the level of our life together, a similar wilderness season is at hand. Many of our communions continue to lose members, year after year. Wilderness. And the institution in many places has turned to a survival mode of desperation about "church growth." Wilderness. Can the diagnosis of "clinical depression" be applied to an entire church? If so, we are in the wilderness. (The preacher will now need to image this wilderness experience more concretely. For example, a recent study of a confirmation class from thirty years ago found few of these now forty-something adults still in any kind of relationship with the church. Only

six out of the original fifty-six remain in any connection with the church. The young faces in the old confirmation photo stare out in faithful confidence. One of those faces belongs to someone who now says, "I don't need the church."

2. The idea that Jesus is the bread come down from heaven, offered particularly to a people in this wilderness place still feels absurd. How can this "marginal Jew," as one recent author described Jesus, help us in this location called the wilderness? It is interesting to note the recent concern once more in the historical life of Jesus. The Jesus Seminar, with their different colored beads, vote on whether or not Jesus said or did the things claimed for him and have come to find out that we are left with a Jewish reformer who himself perished in a tragic clash with the powers that be. And if there is only such a wilderness location for Jesus—not just the forty days at the beginning of his ministry, then how indeed can he say, "I have come down from heaven"?

3. Of course, the outcome is that we too perish, get lost out here in the wilderness and perish. We hunger for righteousness and the poor remain violated and exploited. (Provide an image here.) We hunger for some sense of wholeness within ourselves, but in the wilderness all those shelves of self-help books at the local book superstore just mock us with their upbeat slant on things. (The image here could be one of standing at those shelves leafing through a book, maybe with a chapter titled "Finding the Real You!") And as for the church, for our community of faith, many of us have been out here in the wilderness for so long that, like our ancestors, we murmur and complain. (Once more, an image is needed. Perhaps a reference to the way anger can float around in the church.) To distract ourselves and numb the pain we turn to an addiction of one sort or another. Perhaps there is no more compelling symptom of our wilderness location than the way we have chained ourselves to the insatiable hunger of addiction. Always hungering, we give away our freedom, too, out here in the desert.

4. Now to all of us out here in the wilderness, hungering and about to perish, the word comes from this "marginal Jew": *Egō eimi*, we hear; "I am . . . bread of life." And with that word tumble out others, ones about our not being driven away because we have complained, about no longer hungering for bread, and about the gift of eternal life. So now there is a clash of images, each dealing with either death or life, hunger or feeding, perishing or being found. Juxtaposed with this image of ours of a marginal Jew is that of the icon of the resurrection. In the icon, to the right of the altar screen in every Orthodox church, is the risen Christ just come out of his tomb at Easter. And as he is about to be lifted up, he first lifts up old Adam and Eve out of their coffins to each side of the now-empty tomb. And we look down and peer into the abyss there under the thin slice of earth on which the coffins had reposed. Bits of chains and broken locks are falling into the Pit! Amazing. It is not ourselves who are plunging into that nothing place, but the chains of our bondage. And the words again echo through the wilderness, "Whoever eats this bread will live forever."

Thirteenth Sunday after Pentecost
Twentieth Sunday in Ordinary Time
Proper 15

Lectionary	First Lesson	Psalm	Second Lesson	Gospel
Revised Common	I Kings 2:10-12; 3:3-14 or Prov. 9:1-6	Psalm 111 or Ps. 34:9-14	Eph. 5:15-20	John 6:51-58
Episcopal (BCP)	Prov. 9:1-6	Psalm 147 or Ps. 34:9-14	Eph. 5:15-20	John 6:53-59
Roman Catholic	Prov. 9:1-6	Ps. 34:2-3, 9-15	Eph. 5:15-20	John 6:51-58
Lutheran (LBW)	Prov. 9:1-6	Ps. 34:9-14	Eph. 5:15-20	John 6:51-58

FIRST LESSON: I KINGS 2:10-12; 3:3-14

The pericope treats the story of the succession of David's throne to Solomon, undergirding that succession with Yahweh's authorization of Solomon as king. The last two verses of chap. 2 deal both with the death of King David and the accession of Solomon to the throne. David is buried "in the city of David"; Jerusalem will henceforth be know as David's city. As chap. 3 opens, the reader is told some important information about Solomon's character directly by the narrator. Later, the reader will gain additional information indirectly by way of the night revelation of God.

At the outset, however, we are informed directly of Solomon's righteousness—he walked "in the statutes of his father David"—and his piety—"he sacrificed and offered incense at the high places" (v. 3). The latter comment sets up the opportunity for the narrator to tell of a particular journey by the new king to Gibeon, to sacrifice at that principal shrine. The references to the many offerings Solomon had made there (one thousand!) suggests a continuing devotion to God expressed at that chief country shrine. On visit one thousand and one, though, the Lord graces Solomon with an appearance in a dream. We are told that "the LORD" appeared to Solomon, with the name "Elohim" connoting perhaps a more general designation for God. This Elohim asks Solomon to name whatever it is that he wishes to be given. The reply begins with a recital of God's graciousness to his father David, a graciousness that now extends to God's servant upon the throne. Solomon admits to God that he is young and inexperienced ("only a little child") who does not know "how to go out or to come in" (v. 7). In the midst of this recital, we hear Solomon's use of the covenant name of God, Yahweh, in addition to the repetition of Elohim. This naming of the God of Israel then nicely leads to the new king's confession of his place within the covenant—a servant "in the midst of a people you have chosen." (v. 8). Solomon's righteousness, young as he is, already extends to at least this awareness of the role and place of the king in the midst of God's chosen people. From that perspective, Solomon makes his request of God.

Honestly dealing with the enormous challenges of governing the people Israel, Solomon asks God for "an understanding mind, . . . able to discern between good and evil" (lit., "a hearing" or "listening heart"). Because Solomon has asked for such a righteous gift of his God, the narrator injects a comment to the effect that this pleased the Lord. God's message in response is in the form of an address that praises Solomon's virtue and offers him a promise. The request will be granted; the new king will be graced with a God-given discernment and wisdom. Moreover, that which was not requested will also be granted, "both riches and honor all your life" (v. 13). The promise is extended even more, according to Israel's God. There will be no other king who will come up to Solomon with respect to these riches and honor. In fact, hidden within this promise to Solomon is the future destiny of Israel regarding its rulers. The monarchy will reach a high water mark of honor, wealth, and righteousness with Solomon. Israel will remember this reign through the generations, for its glory will remain only that of Solomon the king.

SECOND LESSON: EPHESIANS 5:15-20

In the section of exhortations read last Sunday (Eph. 4:25—5:2), the focus shifted from attention to ethical particulars within the household of faith to more general considerations regarding Christ and the church. In the present text, however, the pattern is reversed, with the more general issue of wisdom and foolishness opening the discussion and more particular exhortations following. The writer of the epistle draws on conventional wisdom tradition distinctions between the wise and the foolish, with the latter most probably referring to those outside the community of faith. This judgment is supported by the encouragement to "redeem the time" in v. 16. (The NRSV's rendition of "making the most of the time" is certainly acceptable, but the more forceful "redeem the time" alternative may function as the better translation.) In either case, we should consider v. 16 as an elaboration of the dichotomy in v. 15 between the wise and the foolish. It is because of the ways the foolish live in the world that the days are evil; given these evil days, there is the opportunity to redeem them within the Body of Christ. The same dichotomy is present in the next verse as well (5:17). Those who are foolish have no understanding of the will of God; in the wisdom tradition this is the root of their evil deeds. If a person is wise, he or she derives that wisdom from an understanding of "the will of the Lord."

The shift in v. 18 is sudden and moves from these general issues to a most particular one of drunkenness with its resultant "debauchery." The admonition resonates with Paul's injunctions against drunkenness in Rom. 13:13 and 1 Thess. 5:7b. Even though this dramatic shift has been made in the movement of the text, the fundamental dichotomy still remains that of the unwise and the wise, the worldly and the being saved (see 1 Cor. 1:18-25 for Paul's more extensive dealings with this dichotomy). Once more our writer surprises us with the binary opposition. The reader is predisposed by the admonition against drunkenness to expect an encouragement towards sobriety. Instead, the alternative to being satiated *with* wine is to be filled *by* the Spirit (*en pneumati*). In the former, it is the person who indulges who becomes filled, in the latter, the Spirit is the active agent, filling the believer. Both conditions, notice here, result in profoundly social manifestations. Those filled with wine gather in debauchery, while those filled by the Spirit gather for worship. Neither is simply an individual activity; there are communal consequences to individual conditions that represent foolishness or wisdom.

The Spirit-filled worship that springs up from Spirit-filled worshipers is described in much the same way as in Col. 3:16b. These "psalms and hymns and spiritual songs" are most likely the kind of rich hymnody found in various locations in the New Testament. And while these canticles and hymn texts draw deeply on the Hebrew Scriptures for their imagery and organization, the early Christian liturgical use of the Book of Psalms remains unclear. What is clear, however, is that the writer of Ephesians is encouraging practices that mark the ongoing liturgical life of that church. With this in mind, the intent of v. 19b should not be read as shifting the focus back to the individual and thereby away from the community. Rather, the reference to singing and melody-making "in your hearts" is a way of inviting believers to Spirit-filled worship that is external, yet also within and from the heart. The concluding line also parallels the structure of Col. 3:16-17 with an encouragement to the faithful to "give thanks" (*eucharistoutes*). Thanksgiving, therefore, unites the general and particular foci embodied in the pericope. The general elements refer to thanksgiving "at all times and for everything." But that same thanks is precise and particular as well—it is offered "to God the Father" and is always given "in the name of our Lord Jesus Christ." By way of this thoroughly biblical particularity, once more the community of faith is distinguished from the world, from those who fill themselves only with wine and whose ways are debauchery and foolishness.

GOSPEL: JOHN 6:51-58

Within the Bread of Life discourse two dominant references to the image have persisted, the sapiential, or wisdom understanding and the eucharistic. If the former claimed the foreground in 6:35-50, now the focus in vv. 51-59 is clearly on the latter. The *ego eimi* announcement is restated, this time as "living bread" in an obvious parallel with the "living water" of 4:10-11. The parallels extend through affirmations that to drink and eat this living water/bread is (*a*) to be graced with eternal life and (*b*) to have that gift offered to "the world" (explicitly in 6:51 and implicitly in chap. 4 as that gift is offered to Samaritans). And in both cases water and bread, obstacles and even scandals, obstruct the path that leads to life.

The obstruction to belief appears first in the statement that Jesus' bread given for the world is his flesh (*sarx*). The word is shocking in its direct violation of Jewish sensibilities and ritual prohibition. Consequently, the hearers "disputed among themselves" concerning this saying. (Raymond Brown interprets the Greek here as suggesting "a violent dispute" [*GAJ*, 282]). Jews do not eat human flesh, it is a practice forbidden by God. They therefore enter into a violent dispute. But in v. 53, Jesus provides another level to the deepening scandal by stating that "unless you eat the flesh of the Son of Humanity and drink his blood, you have no life in you" The conventional word for "eat" is not used here; *trōgōn* (v. 54) suggests the kind of eating done by animals similar to the distinction in German between *essen* and *fressen*. The trajectory continues to deepen the opposition to belief—believing in Jesus involves true seeing, being drawn to him, and eating his flesh and drinking his blood. For the believer, then, no part of him or herself can remain "apart" from Christ if the gift of living bread is received. The other side of the equation is that Christ withholds nothing of himself on behalf of the life of the world. At the living center of the gift of "the living Father"(6:57) is the church's Holy Meal at which the gift is most fully given. Here, the evocative image of Jesus as the bread of life and the graphic implications of "munching flesh" are not as much resolved are brought together in profound mystery.

HOMILETICAL STRATEGIES

1 Kings 2:10-12; 3:3-14. Imagine the sermon as a children's sermon. That the adults in the congregation are allowed to "overhear" is possible, too. But to tell the story to children is in keeping with the text; Solomon, after all, identifies himself to God as "only a little child." Begin with a description of "Solomon in all of his glory." A tally of all of the king's chariots, riches, and international dealings, however, cannot remain past tense. Therefore, you may want to contemporize a bit here. Tell all of us "kids" just how wealthy and respected Solomon would be if he lived today. How would that be described? Would Mercedes limos be pulling into and out of his residence, with ambassadors from who-knows-where? And how would we hear the wealth of this king described in such a way that "filthy rich" most certainly does not come to mind? We will need to hear of his reputation, too, one of honor and integrity. Which public figures can serve as analogies at this point? And we will be told of Solomon's favor with God, but that is where we begin the flashback to the story in the text.

We begin with young Solomon worshiping at the shrine at Gibeon. What is noteworthy about this is first that he already is deeply formed in the habit of prayer and the practice of worship of the God of Israel. Apparently nothing out of the ordinary happened through one thousand visits to the holy place; Solomon simply worshiped faithfully the God of his ancestors. It was only on occasion one thousand and one that there is an appearance by God to Solomon while he slept at the shrine. The word to Solomon is amazing and straightforward: "Ask what I should give you." Now is the opportunity to "ask" the children who are the sermon's implied audience how they would answer God's offer. Equally important, it would be instructive if these "children" were asked how their parents would respond to such a night vision. By the conclusion of these explorations, we should have in front of the congregation a pile of stuff that Solomon in all his glory could only dream about! Our answers to the offer by God should not present a stereotype of greed. Rather, the preacher could simply inventory the products and services offered through one evening's viewing of commercial TV. Of course, all of these acquisitions are geared to render us healthy and wealthy, but not wise.

Now it is precisely what our culture does not value—this wisdom—that is the content of Solomon's request to God. And notice that the kind of wisdom requested is of a practical sort, the kind of wisdom needed to govern "a great people." So we will now hear in this "children's sermon" the kind of practical wisdom needed to help people in their struggles for a decent life today. What does this kind of wisdom look life? Remember to keep the examples well imaged and unladen with ideological slogans—we are telling a children's sermon, remember? Perhaps the kind of wisdom God will grant Solomon will help him organize a Habitat for Humanity in our community so people won't have to be homeless or live in terrible conditions. A brief description of "wise Solomon" supervising the work project would be helpful so the "kids" could see this wisdom in action. Other kinds of practical wisdom projects could be envisioned in a similar way. (A caution to preachers: Avoid doublet illustrations here. Two examples illustrating a single meaning in a sermon will weaken analogy and get in the way of hearing. Either stick with one clearly imaged example or go for three or more.)

Now is the time to hear God's promise of abundance precisely because, God tells the king, he has not "asked for [him]self long life or riches." These are now promised as well as honor. Solomon will always be remembered as Israel's most glorious ruler: "No one like you shall arise after you," God announces in the dream. So now the preacher can remind all of us of the glories of Solomon recounted at the beginning of the sermon. But perhaps the sermon should end with the image of the young king getting ready once more to worship God. He might entertain the thought that after a thousand times of worship, maybe he could just skip this worship number 1001 and sleep in or go play. "No," Solomon probably thinks, "God loves me this day too and I will go to the house of the Lord."

Ephesians 5:15-20. The pericope is characterized by a persistent dialectical argument presented to "redeem the time." Drawing on the wisdom tradition, the writer of the Epistle distinguishes between the foolish and the wise, the latter understanding the will of the Lord for their lives. The former fill themselves with wine for debauchery while the wise are filled with the Spirit. If the works of the foolish and drunken ones are degraded and selfish, the fruits of the Spirit's indwelling centers most fully in eucharistic worship, singing heartily to God the Father "in the name of our Lord Jesus Christ." The homiletical challenge here is twofold: First, there is a danger that the "foolish-drunken-debauched" lifestyle of these evil days will be brightly and concretely imaged while the Spirit-filled and eucharistic praise of the wise will only be talked about in generalities. Second, while being faithful to the text's dialectic, we will need to avoid any kind of binary sermon structure that shifts the congregation's attention back and forth between the wise and the foolish. Such rapid and frequent shifts in point of view will only boggle the community's consciousness of the sermon. Given these cautions, we may sketch out a homiletic plot that proceeds with the following moves or locations:

1. Look at the foolish, they care only for themselves and not at all for God's will. The focus here is on the radically self-centered way of life of the foolish. Some in-depth diagnosis of our culture's narcissism is called for here. An illustration, perhaps from a recent film, may be utilized.

2. And look at the kinds of living that result from such foolishness. "Drunkenness" becomes the metaphor for all kinds of behavior that attempts to satiate the self above all. We may certainly speak of and image actual drunkenness, but we may also provide examples from such disparate places as the most recent scandal in government or our local casino.

3. But we are filled with the Spirit, God's holy people. There is a trajectory in this text of Scripture between the gift of the Spirit to the believer and the discernment of God's will. While the gift is of God's grace, our response includes using the gift to discern God's will. The process is both profoundly personal and communal. How to image this mystery is the challenge of the sermon. The coordinates of the imagery are (1) gift of the Spirit–discernment of God's will and (2) personal–communal.

4. So rejoice and sing. Give thanks together to our God! Sing and make melody to the Lord. Here the imagery may derive quite directly from the liturgy within which the sermon is preached. In planning for this Sunday, perhaps the musical leadership of the community could provide a "congregation and choir" sung act of praise that will follow immediately upon the sermon. Or there may be a particularly festive musical setting for the eucharist as well. At any rate, the sermon should end in celebration and with an invitation to God's people all to join in that praise!

John 6:51-58. The latter portions of John 6 leave behind the narrative textures of the earlier material in the chapter almost completely. Now, we are hearing a discourse with the disputes of "the Jews" serving as a foil to propel the self-revelation of Jesus. In place of full-blown narrative, the pericope deals in the strongest imagery imaginable. A sermon based on this lection, therefore, might be ordered by the image system that dominates the text rather than a more formal narrative plot.

Imagine this sermon as composed of an introduction dealing with the context of the discourse and what follows as a sequence of brief narratives all attending to the image of Christ as "living bread." The stories need not relate to each other directly; in fact, if they share too much in content they will blur together in the congregational hearing. So, for example, we would not want to include several stories that had in common references to "a young man" or "a little child." What is intended here is a sequence of image-based stories that will resonate within the communal consciousness of the hearers. The effect should be much like that of a series of transparencies overlaid on a projector. Again, the homiletical "glue" of the sermon is not a narrative plot but the biblical text's image-system that will relate to all of the stories in succession. Some possible narratives for this image-based sermon are listed below. You may want to add to these suggestions or exchange them for stories of your own.

1. The story of manna in the wilderness (Exod. 16:11ff.) may be told. If the other stories are related in the present tense, keep this one in the present as well. As with all the stories in this sequence, you may want to build a tag line such as "So Jesus speaks to his church: 'I am the living bread,' He says, 'come down from heaven.'"

2. A story of a divorced man or woman (you will need to decide gender here) who has refrained from communing since the breakup of the marriage. There has been shame and guilt along with a feeling of being "outside" the church family. But now the decision is made and he or she (again, decide which) is walking down the aisle, hands open to receive the living bread, come down from heaven.

3. The cheery church treasurer dishes out heaping plates of spaghetti for hungry and homeless folks gathered at the church's Drop-In Center. Every week over one hundred people find warmth and welcome and a good homemade meal. As the pastor comes by with (her/his) plate at the end of the line, the treasurer beams. "Just like loaves and fishes, eh, Rev?" "Yes," (she/he) thinks, "just like loaves and fishes."

Fourteenth Sunday after Pentecost
Twenty-First Sunday in Ordinary Time
Proper 16

Lectionary	First Lesson	Psalm	Second Lesson	Gospel
Revised Common	I Kings 8: (1, 6, 10-11), 22-30, 41-43 *or* Josh. 24:1-2a, 14-18	Psalm 84 *or* Ps. 34:15-22	Eph. 6:10-20	John 6:56-69
Episcopal (BCP)	Josh. 24:1-2a, 14-25	Psalm 16 *or* Ps. 34:15-22	Eph. 5:21-33	John 6:60-69
Roman Catholic	Josh. 24:1-2, 15-18	Ps. 34:2-3, 9, 16-23	Eph. 5:21-32	John 6:60-69
Lutheran (LBW)	Josh. 24:1-2a, 14-18	Ps. 34:15-22	Eph. 5:21-31	John 6:60-69

FIRST LESSON: I KINGS 8:22-30, 41-43

The dedication of the temple has concluded with the transfer of the sacred utensils and the elaborate gifts deriving from David's conquests and David's reign. But it is the temple of Solomon, and he is the one who had the temple built and who has the ark of the covenant brought in and installed in its place between the cherubim. Glory then appears in the form of a cloud such that the priests must leave their posts and Solomon must turn his face away from the Presence. Now the formal dedication occurs, gathered into three distinct sections in chap. 8. In the first (vv. 14-21), Solomon addresses the people whom he faces, providing a rationale for the Davidic line and succession in the form of a blessing of God. The middle section of the dedication (vv. 22-29) begins the formal prayer and focuses on praise and on consideration of the mystery of the glory of Israel's God, both manifest at the temple yet filling the heavens. In the final section (vv. 30-61), the prayer turns to intercession proleptically for certain special situations that will be brought to the temple for resolution and concludes with doxology. The lection itself picks up only the last of these intercessions, dealing with the place of foreigners in this place of Israel's God.

At the opening of the prayer of dedication (v. 22), Solomon stands facing away from the temple and extends his arms in prayer to God. The opening address acknowledges the singularity of Yahweh, God of Israel; "there is none in heaven above or earth beneath," Solomon proclaims. The God of Israel is One who keeps covenant (*berith*) and steadfast love (*hesed*) to all those who have been chosen and walk as servants before the Lord. Yahweh is also a God of promise, especially noted in the prayer on the day when what God had promised to David is now fulfilled in the completion of the temple. The prayer retains its attention to David, now praising the Lord for the promise of succession to David's throne, providing the faithfulness of the people toward their God remains (v. 25). Verse 26 represents a kind of epiclesis of the Word, enacting now the promise made the David: "Let your word (*dabar*) be confirmed."

Upon the completion of that dedicatory word-event, Solomon now turns in prayer to consider the glory of God that fills the entire heaven, and "heaven's heaven," yet deigns to make abode in this house. "But will God dwell on the earth?" Solomon asks, and humbly petitions exactly that of God. The balance is nicely retained, however. Solomon never asks of the Lord to dwell in the temple by vacating heaven or elsewhere on earth. The prayer continues to address the God of Israel, God of heaven and earth, requesting the fulfillment of the promise, "My name (*shem*) shall be there" (v. 29). The dwelling place of God remains in heaven, yet Solomon makes bold request that the Lord far removed hear the prayers of the faithful when they pray "toward this place" (v. 30). Solomon concludes this section with a priestly petition: "Heed and forgive."

The petition that the Lord God receive the prayers of the faithful when prayed "toward this place" (v. 30) now sets up the occasion for Solomon to propose certain specific kinds of requests that may very well be addressed toward this place. A series of prolepses are stated, each portraying a situation and then requesting the Lord to hear and act in a certain way: hence, when Israel is defeated in battle, or to restore the land that God had promised when afflicted with drought, pestilence, or locusts, and to relieve those plagues. The lection includes only the last of these anticipated conditions, now raising even the foreigner who comes and prays in this house. The prayer anticipates that this shall be a house for all peoples and nations, and that the righteous shall come from afar to worship the God of Israel. When that future comes to pass, Solomon prays that God will hear the prayers of even these foreigners. The proleptic vision here is once more stated in the form of prayer—"that all the peoples of the earth may know your name and fear you, as do your people Israel" (v. 43). The dedicatory prayer, therefore, both stands as a charter for the temple's present purposes and as a vision of humanity's fulfillment in worshiping the God of Israel in Zion.

SECOND LESSON: EPHESIANS 5:21-33

The "household rules" section of the epistle deals with the nature of marriage within the new community in Christ. Its Christ–church/husband–wife analogy along with the notion of the "subordination" of the wife to the husband has led many, including the drafters of the Revised Common Lectionary, to simply excise this material from the readings for the Lord's Day. Both the notion of wifely "subordination" as well as the metaphor of the church as the bride of Christ are regarded in many circles as hopelessly culture-bound and oppressive to women. The response, therefore, is to delete the text from any hearing except in a derogatory context. What is unfortunate about these attitudes and actions is that it is precisely Eph. 5:21-33 which stands in strongest opposition to any sexism attempting to justify itself on the basis of the argument in that text. In fact, the pericope may well wind up being profoundly countercultural in its "household rules"—both to first-century Ephesus and to contemporary America.

In keeping with Pauline practice, the writer of Ephesians treats the "weaker" member of a set first, in this case wives. They are to "be subject" to their husbands "as you are to the Lord" (5:22). The authority for this culture-bound admonition is the analogy between Christ and the church—Christ is its head, the husband, therefore, "the head of the wife" (v. 23). The role and status of the wife derives from the order of redemption, then, and not—in this epistle—from the order of creation. What is frequently overlooked is the far greater attention accorded to husbands. They are to love their wives (*agapate*) in a way analogous to Christ's love for the church, even to the point of emulating the kind of self-sacrifice Christ made for his church (v. 25b). Moreover, husbands are to love (*agapan*) their wives in the same way they love their own bodies. The force of the argument reverses itself in v. 28b: "He who loves (*agapōn*) his wife loves (*agapa*) himself." These affections and actions of wifely "subjection" and husbandly love are focused in an implied "bride of Christ" image, in which the church is presented as made holy by Christ and presented to Christ in splendor (v. 27).

Woven through this argument, however, are strands of Christology and ecclesiology that create a new garment (to borrow another Pauline image) and that invite the culturebound to see "a still more excellent way" (1 Cor. 12:31b). Interestingly, the image of the cleansing bridal bath is elaborated with reference to baptism in Christ—"the washing of water by the word" (v. 26). Two distinct shifts in meaning occur by virtue of this introduction of the metaphor of baptism. First, baptism is offered to women and men, slave and free, Greek and Gentile, that is, to all who seek faith. Whatever the "household rules" for wives and husbands who are members of the body, there is in Christ a new location of equity within the household accompanied by an insistence on the need for the holiness of all within the body. The shift from bridal bath to baptismal washing by the word achieves something else as well. Baptism, as one commentator has put it, "continually incorporates new people into the Church"; the making of this splendor is "a present and continuing event" (Schnackenburg, 1991, 251). The metaphor of the bridal washing as a unique event is shattered. Only brides take bridal baths; husbands and wives both wear their baptismal garments, signs of holiness, equality, and Christ's self-giving love. Of course, if the countercultural weight of this argument should be missed by some, the writer offers the conclusion for wives and husbands at the first: "Be subject to one another out of reverence for Christ" (v. 21). That opening conclusion cannot be reached by way of oppressive subordination and domination. Maybe that is why the writer placed the conclusion first.

GOSPEL: JOHN 6:60-69

The concluding section of the Bread of Life discourse embodies two contrasting dynamics, one related to Jesus and the other pertaining to the hearers. Both movements are initiated by the complaint of "many of his disciples" that the teaching about Jesus as bread of life is a "hard word" (*sklēros logos*). Jesus, aware of this complaining by his followers, asks them directly, "Does this offend you?" (*skandalizei*). On the heels of all the scandalizing words—especially those about eating the flesh and drinking the blood—now a pair of movements are seen. First, Jesus announces the coming ascension of the Son of Humanity, which is intimately linking with the descent of the Spirit. Implied here is the theological perspective of the Fourth Evangelist, that as Jesus is lifted up on the cross, so he is also lifted up in glory. This simultaneous "lifting up" then makes possible the gift of the Spirit upon those who believe, a Spirit that brings life. (That gift of life does not occur at Pentecost for John, but is bestowed immediately upon the disciples gathered behind locked doors on Easter evening.) Now, the Spirit's gift of life is promised as a finale to the entire Bread of Life discourse.

The other dynamic pertains to those who have heard all these "hard words." Prior to the discourse, we have already learned of the opposition and disbelief of "the Judeans," for example, in 5:16ff. Within the sweep of the discourse itself, however, disbelief and opposition are intensified in both scope and consequence. The crowds, who have come to Jesus to see signs and be filled with bread, complain and dispute over Jesus in the face of his self-revelation and offer of living bread. And in the face of the scandalous words of Jesus, now "many of his disciples turned back and no longer went with him" (6:66). The focus now draws in on the Twelve, and even here there is profound opposition—noted in the betrayal of Jesus by that devil Judas in vv. 70 and 71. This dynamic of denial, however, exhausts itself with Judas. Peter speaks for the others in response to Jesus' question, "Do you also wish to go away?" His answer names Jesus as "Lord," states that "You have the words of eternal life," and confesses, "you are the Holy One of God" (*ho hagios tou Theou*).

Peter's question, "Lord, to whom shall we go?" however, propels the dynamics of belief and unbelief beyond the context of the synagogue discussion in Capernaum. It is to the reader of the discourse that these words have also come, to those who hear them gathered together on the first day of the week. All who hear these hard words, notice, have already been fed by Jesus, the bread come down from heaven. From a "fleshly" point of view (v. 63) all who eat bread will hunger again, and will die. From the vantage point of belief energized by the Spirit, those who munch on Jesus' flesh and drink his blood live forever. And in answer to Peter's question, the faithful hearers will respond, "No, Lord, there is no one else whose words bring life."

HOMILETICAL STRATEGIES

1 Kings 8:22-30, 41-43. Solomon's prayer reflects a series of relationships being established with the new temple, a series of movements toward it. The first, and most decisive, is Solomon's petition that the God of Israel become present within "this house that I have built." The prayer acknowledges that all of heaven and earth cannot contain the fullness of God, yet reminds God of the promise that "My name shall be there." With regard to homiletic strategy, then, a first section of the sermon may explore this mystery of God whose glory cannot be contained in heaven and earth yet comes down to dwell among us. To the question, "Will God indeed dwell on earth?" the covenant community in Christ responds with joy at the mystery and sings, "Christ our God to earth descendeth, our full homage to demand."

The second section of the sermon may now focus on the congregation itself, "your people Israel when they pray toward this house." There is movement implied here as well and at least on two levels. First is the wonder of God's faithful people renewing covenant week in and week out by gathering together for worship in the name of Christ. This is a deeply moving drama now reenacted by those who are participating in the liturgical act of the sermon along with the preacher. This faithfulness should be celebrated both today and within its context in the biblical tradition. We now stand in a line of worshipers of the God of Israel extending back to Solomon and that congregation on the day of the temple dedication. But there is a second movement implied here as well. As the people draw near to pray, Solomon asks that God will "heed and forgive." That second movement occurs, therefore, by way of confession, pardon, and reconciliation. Without this latter dynamic of metanoia, the business of "coming to church" is only a formality. Both levels are involved in the worship of the God of the covenant, both on that day of dedication and yet again this Lord's Day.

The final movement anticipated in the prayer relates even to those foreigners who will draw near by faith to God. Solomon's prayer envisions that all peoples of the earth will know the name of the Lord and worship the God of Israel. The sermon may have as its last major section some attention to the issues of evangelization and hospitality that are so instrumental in determining whether this vision of Solomon's will come to pass for our community of faith. There is not an "Amen" after Solomon prays for the faithful of Israel. Rather, the prayer continues and anticipates that the foreigner, too, will find forgiveness and healing in the house of the Lord. Our worship both extends back in the tradition to those who first worshiped with Solomon on that dedication day and forward to encompass the stranger, the foreigner, and even the unbeliever.

Ephesians 5:21-32. Based on our interpretation of the pericope, a sermon could move in sequence from "wedding shower" to "baptismal bath." A succession of moves or locations could lead the hearers from traditional attitudes toward marriage based on this text—along with conventional reactions to those traditional attitudes—to a celebration of the equity of marriage in Christ. The homiletic strategy will be shaped as well by pastoral considerations related to convictions held by the hearers concerning marriage and this traditional text. Strong resistance about wifely subjection to the husband will be a barrier to later admonitions concerning husbandly love of the husband for the wife. Both roles, as we have seen, are overcome and transformed by the introduction of the baptismal metaphor in the Ephesians text. Still, the preacher may have to deal with hardened assumptions as to the meaning of the text and its implication for marriage. A successful homiletic strategy here is one that takes this resistance into account and also surprises the hearers with the radical equity inherent in the baptismal character of Christian marriage.

The moves or locations may be plotted as follows:

1. "Be subject," we hear, and many of us react. "No way!" we say. (Or "Says the world!")

Here we will need to speak the resistance of the hearers. We, and the text, will not given a hearing unless we adopt a strategy that acknowledges a stereotyped conclusion concerning the text. Images related to this stereotype are easy to come by. Perhaps the "Cleavers" are now overdone. But examples of resistance to the presumed message of the text abound in church and culture. If such stereotypes are not the dominant obstacle to hearing the text, then the point of view would shift to the stereotypical reading of the text by the world.)

2. But wait a minute, listen to everything a husband has to do, all of it spelled L-O-V-E.

Can a husband "dominate his wife" and still show agape love? Can a husband abuse or ignore his wife and this Christ-love be present? Now the preacher will need to develop a series of examples—perhaps drawn from the wedding vows—of how this husbandly love is lived out in a covenant marriage.

3. Then things shift . . . from wedding showers to baptismal bath—woman and man both washed of water by the Word.

Perhaps both bride and groom should come forward in the white of their baptismal robes to join in holy narriage. Still wet with the waters of their baptism, glistening with the oil of baptismal anointing, they have just heard that in Christ there is neither male nor female but a new creation in Christ. The baptismal context for the marriage covenant does not much support the old "giving away of the bride" from one male to another.

4. Turns everything on its head, marriagewise. Baptized into the servant Jesus, wife and husband are now servants to each other . . . "out of reverence to Christ."

It is increasingly the practice that the eucharist is celebrated at Christian weddings, as it should be. And with that renewal of the rite has come the possibility of bride and groom turning from the vows spoken to each other and serving the gifts to the assembly. Other images of mutual servanthood in Christ may be substituted or added to this central sacramental image.

John 6:60-69. The old hymn sings, "Trust and Obey." Here at the end of the Bread of Life discourse, a countersong has emerged, "Unbelieve and Betray." It is the preacher's task in preaching the Gospel lesson to rehearse the "hard words" of Jesus that were, and are, a scandal for so many, and, in doing so, to offer life. At the center is the "I am" announcement of Jesus as the bread of life. Clustered with this core image are those of the gift of the Spirit and life and the identity of Christ as the coming Son of Humanity. Thus, the memory of Israel is transformed—that is, the true manna from heaven is revealed to be Jesus—and so is its hope—now disclosed as Christ being "lifted up." In between memory and hope, we thirst and hunger, and Jesus offers himself to feed us by munching his flesh. Hard words indeed!

Utilizing the image of feeding as a device to provide sequence and order to the homiletical plot, we could shape a sermon that clustered attention as follows: "Fast food"→"cafeteria"→"checking the menu"→"banquet?" "Fast food" obviously speaks of the lifestyle of the prevailing culture and our biological need for food. Busy-ness, being spread too thin, life lived in low-grade anxiety, "fast food"—they all go together. After developing the endless cycle of this way of life, along with its unhealthy consequences, the sermon then proceeds to the "cafeteria." Here is where the world would like to locate Jesus, in a "pick and choose" arrangement of all the culture's gods and goddesses. The preacher now can image a variety of trays piled up with all sorts of "goodies" along with a side order of belief in Jesus. (Remember, here, we cannot simply stereotype "those other poeple." All of us show up at the cultural cafeteria—liberals pick and choose items from the world religions salad bar and an entree of the latest cultural movement while evangelicals will, of course, select Jesus but also a large cake for dessert iced with the American flag. Do all of us line up and pick and choose? You betcha!)

The next movement of the sermon is the invitation to the banquet in the kingdom. First, we are given a menu featuring the bread of life. Other images from the entire sweep of John 6 may be listed for the congregation as well. Perhaps as we are considering what is really offered to us, our waiter returns, now girded with a towel and kneels and washes our feet. Some will close their menus and leave, the "hard words" and this servant-Lord being too much of a stumbling block. Then the words come to us: "Do you also wish to go away?" Roughly translated, Jesus is asking if we want to go back to fast food and the cafeteria. With what belief we can muster, our response may be that of Simon Peter: "Lord, to whom can we go? You have the words of eternal life." For those who now remain at the table, a banquet is given with Christ at its center. Image this perhaps as a wedding banquet, a family reunion, or maybe "dinner on the grounds"; draw from a gala occasion out of the lived experience of the congregation. And be sure to have eveyone serving as well as being served!

Fifteenth Sunday after Pentecost
Twenty-Second Sunday in Ordinary Time
Proper 17

Lectionary	First Lesson	Psalm	Second Lesson	Gospel
Revised Common	Song of Sol. 2:8-13 or Deut. 4:1-2, 6-9	Ps. 45:1-2, 6-9 or Psalm 15	James 1:17-27	Mark 7:1-8, 14-15, 21-23
Episcopal (BCP)	Deut. 4:1-9	Psalm 15	Eph. 6:10-20	Mark 7:1-8, 14-15, 21-23
Roman Catholic	Deut. 4:1-2, 6-8	Ps. 15:1-5	James 1:17-18, 21-22, 27	Mark 7:1-8, 14-15, 21-23
Lutheran (LBW)	Deut. 4:1-2, 6-8	Psalm 15	Eph. 6:10-20	Mark 7:1-8, 14-15, 21-23

FIRST LESSON: SONG OF SOLOMON 2:8-13

The Song of Solomon has long endured the tradition of allegorical interpretation, in Jewish lore as a depiction of the love of Yahweh and the covenant people and in Christian contexts as the love of Christ and his church. More recently, commentators have suggested the book to be, variously, a text for a drama, or a hymnic text used at a wedding or funeral, or a collection of love songs. A traditional within Roman Catholic interpretation and piety is to view the text as a hymn of devotion to the Blessed Virgin Mary. More recently, however, interpreters are increasingly moving away from allegory as a hermeneutical key to the book and are treating it as a through-composed poem rather than a collection. It is instructive that within the New Testament—where allegory is understood to be an acceptable means of interpreting the Scriptures—there is no reference to the Song of Solomon. Essentially, the conclusion that is most helpful, and challenging to "spiritualized" approaches to biblical faith, is that the book is a Hebrew love song, sharing features with other such poetic texts in the ancient Near East.

The pericope begins with an "arrival song" motif, with the woman's beloved "leaping upon the mountains, bounding over the hills" (v. 8). The depiction of the beloved as a gazelle or stag is an image familiar to arrival motifs in ancient Near Eastern poetry. Once the arrival is accomplished, however, a second motif is now possible to explore, that of the "invitation." First, the invitation is expressed in a covert and unspoken manner as the beloved only stands outside and gazes at his beloved, hidden by the latticework of the wall. Then, the invitation is given voice in the final four and enduringly beautiful verses of the text. The beloved invites the narrator to arise and come away with him, noting the turning of winter to spring. The images expressing this transition of the seasons begin with the more general, affecting all of nature—rains ending, flowers appearing on the earth, people singing, and the turtle-dove's voice being heard. Then, the sequence of imagery focuses in more on those of a garden, with its figs and vines and fragrance. The sweep is from what is occurring in the creation, to the garden, and then finally within the relationship of love. The image of the fragrance of the blossoms in the garden is picked up again in 7:9b-13, possibly a text in chiastic parallelism with 2:8-13. In the immediacy of the garden with its visual beauty and its sweet smells, the invitation is repeated, "Arise, my love, my fair one, and come away" (v. 13).

SECOND LESSON: EPHESIANS 6:10-20

The admonishments that had as their subject the "household rules" of the community of faith now turn both expansive and combative. This classic text on "spiritual warfare" actually is composed of two main sections, introduced by double-term phrases: "be strong . . . in the strength" (v. 10) and "Pray . . . in every prayer" (v. 18). These intensified phrases are the opening markers for admonitions to be equipped for combat against evil and to be strengthened in that combat by prayer. The writer uses the latter topic to employ Paul's characteristic "Pray also for me" (see Col. 4:3) as a means of shifting the attention of the epistle to its writer and of inviting intercessions for that "ambassador in chains (v. 20).

The larger component of the passage is replete with admonitions to "stand" and with imagery dealing with power. The former term introduces two related metaphors into the conversation: (1) wrestling (a most popular sport in Ephesus) and (2) military dress and battle. The admonition "to stand" is of primary importance for wrestlers—"before anything else" as Chrysostom noted (*Homily on Ephesians*, 23) and is the fundamental capacity needed to defeat the opponent. Likewise, and also noted by Chrysostom in his homily, "to stand" is also "the first thing in warfare."

The dominant metaphor of the text, however, is not that of wrestling but of warfare, a choice dictated to the church by several key considerations. First, the community must struggle to redeem the time because of the evil days in which the church exists (5:16); moreover, these struggles are harbingers of "that evil day" in which the church will also have to stand (v. 13). Present-day struggles with evil are in continuity with the final struggle with evil to occur in God's own time. Second, the metaphors must shift from wrestling to warfare by virtue of ("by vice of"?) the nature of the evil engaging the church. This struggle, the writer proclaims, is much more than a fight against "enemies of blood and flesh" (v. 12)—the entire transpersonal and cosmic dimensions of evil are arraigned against Christ's church. Third, it is precisely the transcendent character of the struggle that leads away from the wrestling metaphor and toward that of warfare. Individuals may wrestle spiritually, an example being Epaphras cited in Col. 4:12 as "wrestling in his prayers." Spiritual warfare, however, includes both the individual and the social, institutional, national, and cosmic dimensions of the struggle. Therefore, we are not surprised that all the references to the equipping of Christians for the battle in the pericope are in the plural.

In order to stand firm, the church is admonished to equip itself with "the whole armor of God" (tēn panoplian tou Theou) for the struggle in both these evil days and the evil day (v. 13). This equipage—"belt of truth," "breastplate of righteousness," shoes to proclaim "the gospel of peace," "shield of faith," "helmet of salvation," and "the sword of the Spirit"—resonates with the portrayal of Israel's God as the warrior for Israel in the Hebrew Scriptures. The one exception among these images is the reference to the "feet" from Isa. 52:7, which pertain to "the messenger who announces peace." The issue for interpretation regarding this imagery has centered recently on the "defensive –offensive" question, with commentators and preachers indicating the essentially defensive nature of the armor with the obvious exception of the sword itself. (The machairan in v. 17 is the short sword of the Roman legionnaire— the sword that takes the battle to the enemy.) What is overlooked in this kind of analysis is that while some of the panoply may be more "defensive" or "offensive," it is all for the purpose, as the epistle states, of standing firm, that is, of prevailing against the evil of these days and of that evil day.

It is instructive that the writer of the epistle did not identify prayer as one image of the armor of the church along with all the other imagery. Rather, the admonition to prayer is separated off for its own treatment. The Christian is to be both watchful, standing alert, and in prayer, for both are needed in these days of struggle. Without prayer, the armor is still inadequate in the warfare against the Tempter and all evil powers. In fact, the relationship between the devil and "his wiles" (v. 11) and the admonition to prayer "in the Spirit at all times" (v. 18) is that without prayerful watchfulness, the church will be open to defeat by the Tempter before the battle can even be fully joined. Lacking prayer, the church will not be able to stand either during these days nor in that evil day. Prayer and watchfulness are the ways in which the church stands, does battle, and awaits the Day of the Lord.

GOSPEL: MARK 7:1-8, 14-15, 21-23

In the midst of an intense and demanding Galilean ministry (see 6:56), Jesus is interrupted by a delegation of Pharisees and scribes who had come from Jerusalem. While the demands of the ministry in Galilee among both Jews and Gentiles had been concerned with healing the many who were sick, raising the dead, and teaching in parables, these Jerusalem dignitaries are concerned not for any of those activities but for the ritual behavior of some of Jesus' disciples. These followers of Jesus were eating with defiled hands (koinais, from koinos, meaning "common" and therefore unclean) and thereby repudiating the "tradition of the elders" (v. 3). What was being ignored by these disciples, then, was the growing case law that sought to "fence" Torah and maintain ritual cleanliness at all times within Jewish life. If the accusers were right in their evidence—that some disciples did in fact, ignore this ritual handwashing—then they clearly were unable to enter the temple itself! However, the Pharisaical movement was extending these cultic proscriptions to all of common life—the covenant people were to maintain purity by avoiding anything "common" (*koinos*) within their common life (*koinonia*). These disciples allegedly were in violation of these proscriptions to the extent that their defilement would infect not only themselves, but their neighbors as well.

Jesus' response to the accusation is direct, not in denial that his disciples did what was claimed, but in challenging the assumptions upon which the attacks were based. Although they may work together for good in other contexts, here in v. 8, there is a clear opposition between the commandment of God (*entolen tou Theou*) and the tradition of people (*paradosin tōn anthrōpōn*). The former, Jesus proclaims, are abandoned in favor of the latter, and Jesus quotes Isaiah in naming such practices as hypocrisy (vv. 6-7). The root of the problem, though, goes deeper than mere hypocritical behavior. A hardness of the heart is likewise revealed as Jesus asks, "Then do you fail to understand?" (v. 18). This verse—omitted in all the Gospel lections—is a critical one for understanding the depth of Jesus' critique of his attackers. To "not understand" is for Mark's story of Jesus one of the primary indicators of hardness of heart, a condition that resists the Gospel and ultimately ends in rejecting God's Son. A person cannot both follow Jesus on the Way and also not understand the radical new nature of the reign of God Jesus proclaims and embodies. From the perspective of the kingdom, though, Jesus' words are in harmony with the commands of God: "It is what comes out of a person that defiles" (v. 20). The acts that violate persons and go against the commandments of God are then listed—Jesus sounds very much like Paul in his listing these vices in vv. 21 and 22. These things originate within the heart and issue forth out of the person as defilement. Neither the notion of defilement nor the importance of holiness are in any way overturned by Jesus. The common life togther, the *koinonia*, is most certainly defiled by what is *koinos*. But what really defiles is what issues forth in action from a person whose heart is hardened. Implied here is an invitation to the Pharisees and scribes come down from Jerusalem to turn toward authentic purity before God, and perhaps follow him along the Way.

HOMILETICAL STRATEGIES

Song of Solomon 2:8-13. How shall we preach a sublime piece of Hebrew love poetry in the church? In days past, the text would have been allegorized somehow or other, with the effect that the poetics of love were almost entirely suppressed. But another question follows: Given that the text is a love poem, why preach about it in the first place? Perhaps it is best simply to have it read as a delightful surprise within the canon or, at most, let singers and instrumentalists put it to music. Theologically, it is difficult to see either law or Gospel in the poem and, without allegorization, it certainly lacks a kerygmatic bite. Still, it is both in our Scriptures and is a reading for this Sunday. The latter decision, to locate the hearing of the poem in the midst of the assembly on the Lord's Day, does provide a certain hermeneutic stance for us hearers. Perhaps it can be preached after all.

One approach to preaching the poem would be to consider its four elements in succession with respect to the character of human love and their analogues to love within the covenant community. Retaining the former prevents us from falling into allegory; including the latter invites the hearers to new insights regarding the love shared in Christ. A first section of the sermon, then, would pick up the initial element of the "arrival motif" in the poem. The beloved's voice is heard and his arrival is distinctly "larger than life." There is a heroic quality to new love, reflected again and again in music and the arts. "Love is a many splendored thing," and one of its splendors is the way we invest in our beloved such heroic qualities. The preacher may now want to invite the congregation to visualize the ways in which we attribute a "larger than life" character to the object of our love. We might also depict the love for Christ and his church shown by those who have recently been initiated into its covenant community. Watch a group of initiates who have made their first *Cursillo* (*Tres Dias*, Walk to Emmaus) and you will see a quite similar kind of fervor and devotion.

The next stage in the love poem which is our lection is that of hidden watching. The beloved has arrived, but does not immediately come into his love's presence. There is a gaze, in silence, that is deeply romantic and filled with possibility. Perhaps in our culture with its "show it all, tell it all" approach to sex and sexuality, this stage of deferred consummation will be considered obsolete. Yet it may well be that the depths of love cannot be experienced without some distance and some devotion. The gaze, when eyes meet eyes and hearts meet hearts, seem almost essential to the fullness of love. Look within the church's life as well. We are recapturing a spirituality shaped by the gaze, whether it be in relation to an icon or other imagery in art or in nature. Not all of the faith is conveyed in words, as central as is the Word for us; there are images of our faith that nourish us and give birth to love.

Now comes the word, "Arise, my love, my fair one, and come away." The word is essential after all. Within all of the expressions of biblical literary forms, including love poetry it would seem, lies a deep structure of call and response. "Arise and come" may be seen as the invitation of Israel's God to a people in bondage in Egypt. It is also this invitation into the promised land and the word of liberation from exile. Lazarus heard a word much like this from behind the thick stone door of his tomb and the disciples in Matthew's story of Jesus hear their Lord give this word on the mountain of transfiguration. It also comes to each of us who love the Lord and who love each other. As preachers, we are now privileged to invite the congregation once more to "arise and come," in faith to our God and in care to each other.

Finally comes the turtledove, . . . and all the other images of the earth are refreshed and made new. The poem now connects the mystery of human love to the order of creation. Now that winter is gone with its rains, all of nature sings, and its song for our poet is a love song! Of course the opposite is true as well. Where hate is the bond between people nature suffers its ravages along with the combatants. But the focus is much more on the resonance between the love humans can share and the ways in which that love extends to the earth and is sung back by the earth. Can the preacher provide a series of scenes in which this shalom extends from covenant love to a care of the earth? And can the preacher also celebrate ways in which the congregants are connecting their love for each other and for Jesus Christ with a love for the earth? Probably. It just might preach after all.

Ephesians 6:10-20. For some preachers, the decision will be made not to preach the Ephesians text because of its use of military imagery. The critique is now held by some that such imagery is to be suppressed entirely within a church committed to peace and justice. This may be a superficial response to the problem of the text's imagery, however. The issues raised within our pericope, and most centrally into the understanding of evil the text conveys, need to be probed more deeply within the American church. All of the imagery related to spiritual warfare is deployed by the writer in the face of evil whose power is both personal and transpersonal, local to our particular human situation yet cosmic in proportions. If sin and evil, on one hand, are pietistically conceived as only at work within the individual human heart, the struggle against it may not require "the whole armor of God." On the other hand, if sin and evil are construed as essentially institutional in nature, then the stance may involve empathy with their victims and confession as to our own complicity in oppression. Neither pole of this dualism, though, adequately grasps the biblical insight into human sin and evil. In fact, both options at large in the church today present only lopsided abstractions of the biblical assessment of the power of evil. In the words of David Buttrick, the former presents the abstraction of human selves without a world and the latter offers a world without selves. It is against the fullness of evil symbolized in the text as both fully personal yet cosmic, however, that the Christian is encouraged to stand and to overcome. We may yet need to preach this text this Sunday.

One strategy for preaching the Ephesians pericope is to begin with reference to some current issue in church and society, perhaps as expressed in a news story. This example needs to be both concrete and immediate to the concern of the congregation. Its presentation will serve as an introduction, an introduction of a real problem that also presents the problem of evil. Now we can move in the sermon to an exploration of how individualism would handle the problem. This approach should not be stereotyped, but expressed with accuracy. What this approach yields, though, is a confinement of evil to the individual heart and the remedy, of course, is to get various persons in a right relationship with God. But the bind is not resolved. We all notice that others are always ready to take the place of any who get saved from their evil deeds. We also notice that evil has a way of infecting social structures and institutions. So the second stage of analysis in the sermon could be to take a look at the rhetoric of "social-*ism*"—Edward Farley's term—in which evil is depicted as institutional in nature. Our originating problem could now be assessed from that perspective. Still, we are not yet to the place where we can make the kind of analysis made in Eph. 6:12. So the third stage of this sermonic analysis takes us to an appreciation of the full-blown nature of sin and evil. This will now need to be imaged in a way that the congregation can see that the two conventional modes of individualism and "social-ism" do not provide an adequate depiction of the pervasiveness and power of evil. Now, however, we have brought the congregation to an even more profound bind . . . how can we, few as we are, face up to this kind of evil in our midst?

It is at this point that the gospel is brought into play, centering in the proclamation of Jesus Christ, raised from the dead. It is in the strength of this power that we are called to stand. The preacher will want to spend some time here in rehearsing the both personal and cosmic nature of that victory of Christ over evil, over sin and death. The image system of the whole armor of God is now introduced and explored. (Notice that to present the imagery before the extent of evil is understood is to provide an answer to an unasked question!) The sermon now can focus first on the defensive character of this spiritual warfare, but will not want to stop there. In the fight against the principalities and powers, the weapons of the Spirit are also offensive in nature. And in the course of the fight, there is always the need for prayer (prayer is not made into a part of the armament of the Christian but undergirds each and all in the fight). Perhaps the sermon will end with the opening issue now represented but in the light of the admonition of the biblical text that we "stand." Just how will Christians stand in this particular fight, local as it may be, but now seeing it in its full cosmic proportions?

Gospel: Mark 7:1-8, 14-15, 21-23. The encounter between Jesus and the Pharisees come down from Jerusalem is a wonderful piece of pastoral theology for the church. At first glance, though, the presenting issue of ritual cleanliness would seem to be far removed from the practical concerns of most Christians. Yet the tension between following "human traditions" while ignoring the "commandment of God" is a perennial issue for the church. Also at stake in the Markan text (though excised in the lection) is the alternative between having a hardened heart or being open to following Jesus along the Way. A sermon working through these issues might follow a homiletic plot like this:

1. There are times when the reign of God in Jesus is abundantly present, when the fruits of the Spirit are ripening in our midst.

Here is the opportunity to celebrate the good works and great signs of Christ's life and work within the church. Just as Jesus is surrounded by those who have been fed and healed, so is the church, when full alive in Christ. We now need to provide examples of these signs of the kingdom in the lived experience of our hearers.

2. Odd, though, how some church folks only see the negative, and respond in anger.

The Pharisees, though, don't see all these signs of the kingdom. In fact, they won't see them because their vision is restricted. They will find something wrong with Jesus, with him or his disciples. Interesting that for some people, the better the church is doing, the harder it is for them to see anything positive. "Majoring in minors" is usually a symptom of a much deeper pathology with Christ's body. We preachers can probably come up with a good illustration of this predictable dynamic in family systems dysfunction!

3. Problem here is a hardened heart, Jesus says. Looking for any place to dump our anger.

The Pharisees are locating holiness in a conformity to a collection of externals. The fundamental issue, Jesus observes, is the heart of the believer. If our hearts are hardened, we may entirely miss the good news and turn the gospel back into law. Look at the church communities today where hearts have become hardened and tests of denominational loyalty override issues of justice and true holiness. A series of examples here come quickly to mind. (Remember that judgment always begins with our own household, so focus first for signs of this hardness of heart within our own communion!)

4. So search down to the heart of things. Become holy there and the whole church will grow in health and in holiness.

The invitation, then, is to repent of any and all hardness of heart. True holiness springs up from a heart that is filled with the Spirit and issues forth in all kinds of goodness. Interesting, too, how infectious this holiness of heart becomes within the household of faith. Oh, there will always be some, "down from Jerusalem." who need to look for negativity. But our call is to attend to our own heart and to encourage each other along the Way. Perhaps we preachers can image the joy of this holiness so vividly that both we and our congregations hear a fresh invitation to follow Jesus and open our hearts to the Spirit that gives life.

Sixteenth Sunday after Pentecost
Twenty-Third Sunday in Ordinary Time
Proper 18

Lectionary	First Lesson	Psalm	Second Lesson	Gospel
Revised Common	Prov. 22:1-2, 8-9, 22-23 or Isa. 35:4-7a	Psalm 125 or 146	James 2:1-10, (11-13), 14-17	Mark 7:24-37
Episcopal (BCP)	Isa. 35:4-7a	Ps. 146 or 146:4-9	James 1:17-27	Mark 7:31-37
Roman Catholic	Isa. 35:4-7	Ps. 146:2, 7-10	James 2:1-5	Mark 7:31-37
Lutheran (LBW)	Isa. 35:4-7a	Psalm 146	James 1:17-22, (23-25), 26-27	Mark 7:31-37

FIRST LESSON: PROVERBS 22:1-2, 8-9, 22-23

Considerable research has provided a wealth of insight into the wisdom litera-ture of Scripture, including the storehouse of wisdom sayings called Proverbs. These sayings reflect a tradition that is inclusive of gender and class and is even global in scope. To the extent that this sapiential tradition does not appear to assume the covenant narrative as its interpretive context, the proverbs are offered directly to everyone. On the other hand, the narratives of the Hebrew Scripture are infused with characters and plots that reflect the proverbial world. Recent research in both scriptural and nonscriptural proverbs has detected certain recurrent forms within which the sayings "mean." We will employ these insights in our analysis of the proverbs chosen for this Sunday's reading.

The entire block of material in Proverbs 22:1-17 deals with the binary sets of rich and poor and wealth and poverty. This collection also introduces a longer section that deals with a person's relationship with God. Within this material, however, there is a remarkable diversity of forms and even theologi-cal perspectives, given the overall unity of themes. The first proverb is in anti-thetical form, with the opposition being established that of "good name," "favor" and "great riches," and "gold." Actually, the underlying structure is even more complex, offering the alternative conditions:

> a good name and rich
> a good name and poor
> a bad name and rich
> a bad name and poor

Having established these antithetical conditions, then, the second proverb in the set is surprising in that it brings together the rich and poor in the aware-ness that "the Lord (Yahweh) is the maker of them all." The Hebrew phrase

translated "have this in common," literally means "meet together" and typically conveys the meaning of "with a purpose." If the purpose of rich and poor
coming together is that the latter borrow or repay the former, then the aware-
ness of their commonality under creation is remarkable. One other context for
the coming together of rich and poor is also possible—their common worship
of the God of the Covenant. Within that context, with its liturgical purpose,
their arriving at a theology of creation that embraces them all is remarkable as
well, but for a different reason.

The two proverbs in vv. 8 and 9 fall within the section dealing with wealth
and poverty and address issues that are causal of the two conditions. The
proverb on injustice (v. 8) manifests a "synthetic" form, structurally. That is,
the saying is given in the "a" phrase but is deepened and intensified in a following "b" statement. Here, the familiar biblical admonition that a person
reaps what he or she sows is given concretion—calamity is the harvest of
injustice. Again, the companion proverb stands in a juxtaposed relationship to
this saying's focus on injustice and its consequences. Now, in v. 9, the "reap-
ing" is mentioned first, with the actions "sown" described in a following
phrase. Here, what is sown is the good work of sharing bread with the poor (by
the wealthy), and the harvest is that of blessing. The form of the proverb is a
familiar one for a biblical people; the "Beatitudes" in Matthew and Luke
exploit the same structure. For those who are wise, and have attended to the
proverbs in all their riches, the life of blessing (being "happy") include the
conditions of wealth, honor within the community ("a good name"), children,
and a joy in knowing the ways of God.

The last two proverbs of the reading for this Sunday after Pentecost are
located within a new section of material introduced in v. 20 by the reference to
the "thirty sayings of admonition and knowledge." These sayings are structurally of a much more direct and injunctive quality, sharing both similar form
and content with the wisdom of Amenemope of Egypt. The injunction itself is
clear and direct: "Do not rob the poor . . ." (v. 22). The modifying phrases
serve to address motivation, "because they are poor," or location, "the afflicted
at the gate." The function is a kind of shorthand, inviting the reader to conclude that there are no circumstances or locations where robbery of the poor is
acceptable. The following verse provides the underlying reason for the injunction; it is the Lord who pleads the cause of the poor. Moreover, the same Lord
"despoils of life those who despoil [the poor]." "If you do not respect the
Lord," the proverb reasons, "you should still respect and not exploit the poor,
because the Lord will judge you without mercy if you do not show mercy." It
is in the enlightened self-interest, therefore, of even the wicked to not exploit
the poor. But those who seek blessing from God will, of course, honor the
poor, for they are within God's special care.

SECOND LESSON: JAMES 2:1-10, 14-17

The pericope dealing with partiality and discrimination, faith and works, is one of the longest sections of all James's letter that remains consistently focused. It follows most directly from the discussion in 1:22-25 regarding those who only hear or both hear and do the word of God. James's rhetorical strategy is at its best in this passage of the letter. The writer invites the readers to imagine a church situation in which two persons appear for worship, one who is very rich and the other, pitifully poor. Whether the readers see themselves as receiving these two worshipers or envision a hypothetical situation not immediately their own is beside the point. In an almost parablelike discourse, James invites the readers to be in that community and to have these visitors appear. "How shall we respond?" is the question. The two visitors are a binary set—representing extremes of wealth and poverty. Describing someone as gold-ringed and splendidly clothed probably brings to mind not only someone who is very rich, but of the aristocracy as well. Privileges accrue to such a person along with the luxury and wealth; he would be treated with deference and would himself defer to few. The poor visitor is not simply one of the many "working poor" of the first century but is described as a *ptōchos*, someone utterly destitute. Except for the issue of the poor person's health not being introduced, James has presented the readers with this sort of hypothetical—"So imagine that one Lord's Day as you are gathering for worship, the rich man and Lazarus show up at your door. Now how do you behave?"

James answers his own question. The readers are invited to see any preference toward the rich man as discrimination, inviting him to "have a seat here, please," while telling the *ptōchos* to "stand there," or "sit at my feet" (v. 3). Not only have distinctions been made clearly in the Lord's house between the two, the readers are now accused of being "judges with evil thoughts" (v. 4). Now comes the retort by the writer of the letter to this infamous hospitality. The poor are chosen of God but have been dishonored by the readers. Notice that this divine choosing is not simply because of their poverty, but because they are "rich in faith" and they receive the kingdom promised "to those who love him" (v. 5). Implied here is the possibility that some who are poor may miss out on this election if they are also poor in faith and if they choose not to love God. The argument in the epistle, while treading a *via media* between Luke and Matthew on the matter of riches and poverty, leans toward Luke. At any rate, the poor should not be dishonored. On the other hand, James points out to the assembly that it is the rich who have oppressed them, asking "Is it not they who drag you into court?" (v. 6). Clearly James's intended readers are not themselves among the upper and privileged classes. Instead, it would seem that they have suffered at the ring hands of these splendidly clothed people! Ironically, the readers do have a bias toward the very rich in spite of this abuse they have received. To discriminate, however, is to sin, for it breaks the royal law (*nomon . . . basilikon*) of Lev. 19:18, "You shall love your neighbor as yourself." The binary pair have achieved their purpose just by showing up at the church door. Discrimination has been shown by the church, God's law broken, and the assembly has fallen into sin.

Now that the scenario has exposed partiality among the faithful, James turns the discussion to that of faith and works. The conclusion—"faith by itself, if it has no works, is dead" (v. 16) is not implying an opposition between the two. Faith and works are not the new binary opposites. What is being stated here is that real faith, living faith, is faith along with works. Dead faith is so-called faith, but without evidence of works. The latter is dead because it is not faith. Once more, how we respond to those in need, to the least of these our brothers and sisters, will determine whether we are alive in faith or dead. Our tongues will give away our lack of faith if we hypocritically say, "Go in peace; keep warm and eat your fill," while not supplying what these poor ones really need. Works of compassion go with faith and are inseparable. To lack the former, the works, is to of necessity lack the latter, a living faith. And the opposite of a living faith is sin, judgment, and no faith at all.

GOSPEL: MARK 7:24-37

Mark now extends the discussion of what is clean or "common" beyond the context of kosher laws and Jewish traditions. Here, in the present pericope, Mark takes pains to indicate at the outset that the woman of Tyre is a Gentile and that her daughter has an unclean (*akatharton*) spirit (v. 25). Clearly, the entire situation is common and defiling, as is the Decapolis encounter with another Gentile, a man with a speech impediment.

In the former story, Jesus is portrayed by Mark as seeking escape from the intensity of the Galilean ministry with its demands for healings and other miracles. He travels to Gentile territory in Tyre, enters a house and desires that no one knows of his presence. His presence does not escape the notice of a Syro-Phoenician woman, however, who approaches him, falls down at his feet, and begs him to heal her demon-possessed daughter. Jesus' response is in the form of an aphorism, about the priority of feeding children over feeding dogs (*kunarion*, "little dog"). Interpreters point to the possibility that Jesus is quoting an as-yet-undetected Jewish saying, while others observe that a "little dog" is used as an idiomatic as well as literal reference in first-century Greek. The latter would therefore be a reference to the woman's tenacity in the face of what would appear to be an insurmountable barrier of gender and ethnicity between this Jewish healer and herself and her daughter. Either way, the woman does remain tenacious for her family and engages in a riposte to the aphorism with her own—"Even the dogs under the table eat the children's crumbs" (v. 28). Her address to Jesus begins with *kurios*, which is weakly translated in the NRSV as "Sir." In this context, "Lord" would probably be more fitting. Responding to the woman's persistence and faith Jesus announces that her daughter is healed. What follows is a mutual leave-taking, the woman from Jesus and to her daughter now well, and Jesus departing from the region itself.

While the mother intercedes on behalf of her ill child who remains at home, in the second of these stories, it is an anonymous crowd who bring the man to Jesus. Once more, Mark provides indicators that the cast of characters are all Gentiles except for Jesus, this encounter taking place "in the region of the Decapolis" (v. 31). In fact, reflecting upon Mark's telling of the two healing stories leads to an interesting question as to the whereabouts of the disciples. Have they not come with Jesus into these unclean, common locations? At any rate, the man presented to Jesus is described as having "an impediment in his speech" (*mogilalon*) rather than being a "deaf-mute." Mark focuses the reader's attention on a series of actions that may well reflect the growing weariness of Jesus in the face both of public demand and growing "hardness of heart" among the people and even his disciples. Taking the man away in private, Jesus performs certain ritual actions of healing and announces, *Ephphatha*, a word that becomes incorporated in the baptismal practice of the early church. Prior to that injunction, however, Mark tells us of Jesus' own inward state as he "groaned" or "sighed deeply" (the word *stenazo* implies more than simply "to sigh"). After Jesus' command to silence, addressed now to everyone, Mark reports the approbation of the crowd to Jesus' ministry: "He has done everything well" (v. 37). We may need to be reminded that the speakers of this accolade are not of Israel but are Gentiles. There is no hardness of heart at all reflected in such words.

The two stories stand in close juxtaposition, and along with one other narrative (Mark 6:53-56) comprise the three healing stories Mark locates between the two feeding miracles. The juxtaposition is provided by Mark through a device perhaps best described as complimentarity. Where one narrative is thick with detail, the other is thinly detailed if at all. So while there is considerable attention to the introductory description of the encounter with the woman of Tyre including the dialogue with Jesus, the healing of the man moves rapidly beyond any attention to the introductory context. On the other hand, Mark provides a great deal of attention to the words and actions of Jesus involved in the Decapolis healing, while with the woman of Tyre, Jesus only says the word and the child is cured. That these narratives are located between the two feeding miracles is of crucial importance for interpreting particularly the questions related to Jesus' conversation with the woman at Tyre. Since the second of the feedings was in Gentile territory—Jesus has not moved from his location in the Decapolis where he healed the man—it cannot be that Jesus refuses to provide a Gentile woman with "bread from the table." Four thousand Gentiles will shortly be welcomed at the table and fed lavishly by Jesus. The disciples, however, will fret among themselves that they only have one loaf with them in the boat (8:11-21).

HOMILETICAL STRATEGIES

Proverbs 22:1-2, 8-9, 22-23. The Book of Proverbs is a collection of Israel's wisdom sayings. They are practical in application and meant to inform the concrete situations of daily life. They are also intended to be cumulative in effect, with the wise person learning the nature of wisdom's teachings throughout his or her life. The challenge for preaching these wisdom sayings is twofold: (1) how to translate specific maxims from the Hebrew Scriptures into our contemporary setting; and (2) how to design a sermon plot that is mobile and performative in nature. Here in our lection three sets of proverbs are selected, we may assume, because of their common interest in the poor. The first of these sets (22:1-2) has the added interest of focusing on the binary opposition of "good name"/"bad name" as well as rich and poor. Moreover, the notion of rich and poor having something "in common" is rich in connotation for the preacher. Perhaps a storytelling sermon might be an appropriate strategy here.

We might design a sermon-story in which someone who is rich and someone who is poor have two encounters that illuminate what is held "in common" between them. The first, as suggested in our interpretation of the text may have to do with the relationship of debtor and loaner. The second, since "the Lord is maker of them all," could be an encounter within a service of worship. Perhaps the biblical tradition conveyed within that liturgical event could invite both the rich and the poor to some metanoia.

Scene 1. We could begin the story sermon with a description of a person in poverty going to a finance company to try for a loan to help stem both daily expenses and some crushing debts. A description of this person (decide on gender and family) might lead to adopting his or her point of view on entering the finance company, including the wait, the invitation by a slick employee to come into one of those little cubicles with a small desk and a couple of chairs. Some time may be spent on the interview with a disclosure to the congregation that the poor man or woman is not giving full disclosure about all that other debt. What the employee does have to disclose is the horrendously high interest rate the company will charge for the loan. The employee will then need to go speak with the manager and after another long wait, the manager comes out from back, announces that the loan is granted and shakes the poor person's hand. This scene could conclude with the poor person's thoughts and feelings as she or he leaves the place.

Scene 2. The churches of one denomination or communion have decided to hold a (district, presbytery, diocese, conference, etc.)-wide worship service to focus on poverty in the community. We can easily describe how things look as people gather at the larger church hosting the event. What happens is, of course, that there is a meeting just a few days later between the poor (man/woman) and the manager. The manager and his family are already in their seats when the poor person and his or her children arrive and take the empty seats next to the manager. Soon the church is packed with worshipers. Both of our characters know they are sitting next to each other, but neither acknowledges the other as the service begins. Now we may start developing what is held "in common" by the rich and poor as they come before the Lord who made them both. Perhaps we can have the first item "in common" be that because of the crowded event, they wind up sharing a hymnbook as the opening hymn is sung. We could also have them use that same book in common as they stand to join in the reading or singing of Psalm 15. The sermon at that liturgy could perhaps be based on one of the other sets of proverbs in our lection. Later in the liturgy they would be invited to share the peace with each other before going forward (or remaining seated) to receive the eucharist, again, "in common." At the conclusion of the worship, the rich man, the manager, might turn to the poor debtor and say, "Why don't you stop back by the office this week? I think I overcharged you on the interest on that loan." And perhaps the poor man/woman might respond, "Thank you. I also have some additional debts I need to list on the application." To resolve that question, the manager might then say, "Well, the money is still yours. I hope it helps."

James 2:1-10, 14-17. The second option for preaching the lections of the day also envisions a liturgical context in which rich and poor gather. The focus here, however, is not on their relationship in common, but rather on how the *koinonia* extends to both. The scenario in James points out the obvious; the assembly shows discrimination *for* the rich and *against* the poor. Another storytelling sermon may well portray this scenario, but this time we might opt for a method that has a narrative plot but is not "preaching-as-storytelling." We may begin the sermon by describing the scene depicted in the epistle, with the context of worship and the arrival of the two visitors. Remember from our explorations of the text that a man who is very rich is suggested along with a person who is among the poorest imaginable. We can proceed to describe the discriminatory words and actions of that religious community. And we can also then respond, preacher and hearers, with some negative reaction to that obvious discrimination. We, within our religious community, are in a homiletical location standing over against that religious community with its discrimination and preference for the rich. Of course, we might then reflect, this stance of ours implies that we are different, that there is not such discrimination or preference among ourselves. An obvious next sequence in the homiletical plot is to image for the hearers a contemporary version of the two who now visit us. Perhaps the poor person is a "bag lady" or brings some other identity fitting to the pastoral context. And the rich man—who would that be for your hearers? At any rate, we might then provide a series of points of view from within the congregation—the thoughts of the members of the church finance committee as the rich man enters, the reflections on the poor person by those whose parents or grandparents worked their own way out of poverty during the Depression, or the attitude of the greeters as they see—and then smell, the two visitors. We would all have to conclude that we may have more solidarity with the cast of characters in the epistle's little drama then with the poor.

The intention of the text is that the assembly shift its point of view from solidarity with the rich man to solidarity with the poor person. Perhaps the contemporary expression of being "dragged into court" by the rich man is "being given a pink slip at work as the company downsizes." Again, how this is imaged depends on the pastoral and social context. What can be imaged is a solidarity with a poor person who is "rich in faith" and who loves God. There will definitely need to be an illustration of such a person, especially in the face of stereotypes of "the lazy poor." Remember, a true story of just one poor person, rich in faith, and loving the Lord will serve to disrupt the conventional perceptions held of the poor. Even better is a story of a family or community of the poor who fit this description. The sermon's plot turns right here. From the perspective of the writer of the epistle, it is the poor who have a special claim on us and who are privileged to be at the center of our worshiping community. We, ironically, become the guests at their worship, dependent on their hospitality. What will those poor ones say as we enter? Will we hear "Stand there," or "Sit at my feet"? Or will we hear those words of special invitation, "Have a seat here, please." The tagline from vv. 14-17 about faith and works may now be brought into play. It fits here naturally. If the congregation is engaging in mission to the poor, those acts of mercy can obviously be celebrated. But the reversal has occurred, and now, in the place of God's reign, we may hear the invitation by the least of these our brothers and sisters to come and worship God in Christ with them.

Mark 7:24-37. The decision to include in the lection two of the three pericopes Mark locates between the two feeding miracles leaves us preachers with a decision. We most probably cannot deal adequately with both the woman of Tyre and the man of the Decapolis and will therefore need to select one as the basis for our preaching. In the hearing of the congregation, however, the first of the two stories will probably evoke the most attention due to the hard saying of Jesus regarding "the dogs." Perhaps this Year A Sunday, if we preach the Gospel lesson, we should stay with our hearers there in Tyre. Given our analysis of the pericope, we might shape a homiletic plot as follows:

1. Here is Jesus, where he shouldn't be. Up in Tyre, among the unclean Gentiles.	All of the conventional wisdom of his people would keep Jesus out of this place. It is unclean, a place of ungodly corruption. Always there are places like that—where we should not be; people like that who are beyond God's grace. There are neighborhoods named "Tyre" in our cities and times when "those people" gather from all over. (We will need to image this place called "Tyre" quite concretely. Where is it, and who is it for our hearers? The place they would not go voluntarily because of its being unclean.) Jesus, of course, goes there.

2. News gets around, even up here. A woman approaches with her plea—a daughter in bondage to evil and sickness.

Interesting that the woman's daughter has an unclean spirit—there in a place called "unclean." Yet she is aware of a different place, of healing and holiness. She asks for this gift from the Lord. In so doing, the woman speaks for all those who find themselves in bondage, and in the grasp of evil. This representative role of the woman might give birth to a set of examples from our lived experience. On behalf of whom does the woman intercede for healing and restoration?

3. Now the words about throwing food to the dogs. Jesus, maybe quoting a proverb from within Israel, raises the question of how far God's reign extends.

In our day, this saying would be politically incorrect. It reflects a prejudice against a group of people whom are assumed to be morally and spiritually inferior. Can Jesus believe this about the woman? If so, how come he will miraculously feed a Gentile multitude in only a few days? Maybe Jesus is purposely reflecting the conventional wisdom here. Maybe he is saying, "Look, everybody knows I'm not supposed to help you." That rings a bell. We share conventional wisdom about who were supposed to help and who we're not. In some states, it is the illegal immigrant who is outside the "safety net." Perhaps there is an image that strikes home with immediacy to the congregation in their context.

4. See her dogged determination! The woman insists on a place under the table, if not at it. Crumbs, at least, if not a meal.

What do you do when you are in this woman's predicament? You beg for grace. Every one of us, not worthy to even gather up the crumbs under the table of the Lord! Yet what kind of faith is there when we hold out an empty hand to Christ, beggars for grace? That's what we are. Even some crumbs of forgiveness and healing would be enough. If the hearers have been formed within a liturgical tradition where a "prayer of humble access" is prayer before receiving the eucharist, we might provide that stance as a example of being beggars for grace. (In the Mass, Catholic Christians pray just prior to communing, "Lord, I am not worthy to receive you, but only say the word and I shall be healed.")

5. Now hear the words of healing, a Gentile child is healed.

But there are no crumbs, the child is healed, restored to her mother. In a short time, this family will be invited to a Meal, loaves and fishes in abundance! No crumbs under the table. Surprise! God's grace if for all and all are invited to the gospel feast. The preacher will need to illustrate this abundant grace of Christ. Point of view is decisive. It is we, the hearers, who are offered this grace. In other sermons, or a different version of this one, we may be called to offer grace to others. But given the movement of this homiletical plot, we are in the role of recipients. The illustration should retain this point of view. (A sermon conclusion may want to celebrate this grace available to all, and may also extend an invitation to the hearers to receive it fresh once more this day.)

Seventeenth Sunday after Pentecost
Twenty-Fourth Sunday in Ordinary Time
Proper 19

Lectionary	First Lesson	Psalm	Second Lesson	Gospel
Revised Common	Prov. 1:20-33 or Isa. 50:4-9a	Ps. 119 or Wis. 7:26 —8:1 or Ps. 116:1-9	James 3:1-12	Mark 8:27-38
Episcopal (BCP)	Isa. 50:4-9	Ps. 116 or 116:1-8	James 2:1-5, 8-10, 14-18	Mark 8:27-38 or Mark 9:14-29
Roman Catholic	Isa. 50:4-9	Ps. 116:1-9	James 2:14-18	Mark 8:27-35
Lutheran (LBW)	Isa. 50:4-10	Ps. 116:1-8	James 2:1-5, 8-10, 14-18	Mark 8:27-35

FIRST LESSON: PROVERBS 1:20-33

Following the title of the collection in 1:1 and a "prologue" in 1:2-7, two sections of instructions are given before the introduction of Woman Wisdom in 1:20-33. The personification of wisdom as a woman serves a unitive function with regard to the teachings of the entire collection of Proverbs; the wisdom she offers is both singular in its unity and collective in its particular applications. Moreover, Wisdom's search locates wisdom as a gift of the Lord rather than a human achievement. Woman Wisdom appears along with the other stock characters of the wisdom tradition—the "simple" or foolish ones and the "wise." The latter category, we discover, comes to include those who are just learning wisdom's ways along with those who have become sages themselves. Even the sage, however, will always have more to learn from wisdom's instruction.

Wisdom's personified appeal in our pericope is carefully structured according to a chiastic pattern with the proclamation of judgment in vv. 26-28 being located at the chiastic center-crossing. The material extending both prior and subsequent to this centerpiece forms parallel themes, thereby unifying the otherwise diverse material. The opening section establishes the motif of a quest by Woman Wisdom, in contrast to the more conventional notion that wisdom is something we either discover on our own or cannot find because of its esoteric quality. No, the poem announces, wisdom can be possessed and is, in fact, offered to those who seek it. Wisdom offers instruction that is public—"at the entrance to the city gates" (v. 21)—and is neither ultimately private nor esoteric. And wisdom is offered to those who have the capability to receive instruction in the ways of God. Therefore, the "simple ones" of v. 22 are not those who are low in mental skills. The word *pethi* suggests "open-minded to a fault." They will believe anything and therefore are persons of naiveté and folly. The issue here is one of character rather than native intelligence.

Wisdom offers her hand (v. 24) to these scoffers and fools but they have spurned all reproof and counsel. The results are predictable and the portrayal of those consequences functions quite similarly to a prophetic oracle. The depiction of the calamity that will engulf the fools resonates with the portrayal of those who reject God's ways as prophesied by Amos, Jeremiah, and Joel. Their ruin is sure and complete. In that time of calamity, they, the fools and scoffers, will search for Woman Wisdom, but they will not find the one who had searched so diligently for them. The charge against those who reject wisdom's ways is twofold: First, they have hated knowledge and, second, they have rejected "the fear of the Lord" (v. 29). Once more it is clear that issues of character and the human will are more at stake than the mental ability to receive wisdom's instruction. The "fear" that is absent from the fools regarding their God should not be taken in the sense of "fearful" or "afraid." The term much more speaks of a piety and reverence that, ironically, releases the wise and the faithful from any fear at all. Rather, those who attend to Woman Wisdom "will be secure and will live at ease, without dread of disaster" (v. 33). The foolish, on the other hand, have already done themselves in; they will suffer the consequences of the path they have chosen and much like the rich man in Jesus' parable in Luke 16:19-31, will wake up only when it is too late.

SECOND LESSON: JAMES 3:1-12

Once more, the writer of the epistle cycles back to deal with the issue of speech within the assembly. That issue—epitomized as "the tongue"—was raised explicitly in 1:26 where the image of the bridle was introduced as well. At a less explicit level, though, the issue of speech within the community was at stake throughout the admonitions in 2:1-17. Repeatedly, how language functions within the church is made to illustrate the dominant topics of preferentiality and faith and works. Still, the movement from the conclusion of the second chapter's continuing attention to faith and works to the third chapter's focus on "the tongue" is jolting. Suddenly, faith and works are left behind and the attention of the reader is now on teachers and their rhetoric.

The opening admonition of the pericope is that not many of the members of the community should become teachers (*didaskaloi*), seeing that they trade in speech for their vocation. Also implied in the greater strictness of their divine judgment is that the teacher within the assembly has as her or his vocation the transmission of the tradition. This special privilege holds with it more accountability as well ("To whom . . ."). As these words were penned, the realization must have come that the writer too was one of these *didaskaloi*, adding, "For all of us make mistakes" (v. 2). The heart of the problem for the writer is that these mistakes in speaking lead inevitably to deeds that are evil, hence, the need to bridle the tongue in order to constrain the body's deeds. Once the image of the bridle is reintroduced, it is expanded in v. 3 and then set aside while two other images are developed—the ship and rudder along with fire and the forest. In the former, the analogy to words and action is that the rudder, as small as it is, can guide the course of even a very large ship wherever the pilot's will directs. So also, James concludes, "the tongue is a small member, yet it boasts of great exploits" (v. 5). The third image in the sequence relates to the potential for a huge forest fire to result from just a very small fire: "And the tongue is a fire," James ominously points out. The three images all function within the same field of meaning—the tongue and its potentially disastrous consequences for action—though each gives attention to a different aspect of the issue. Bridles can direct the horse and rudders can control large ships in ways that are for good or for ill, likewise the tongue. Little fires, though, have potential only for conflagrations; the image emphasizes the negative dimensions of the relationship between speech and action.

As if to expand on the negativity introduced by way of the fire/forest image, James now universalizes the assessment of the tongue. Among the members of the body, it is set as "a world of iniquity" (*ho kosmos tēs adikias*) and the consequences of its evil encompass nature and originate in the fire of hell (v. 6). Now the writer returns to the issue of controlling such a volatile member through a metaphor drawn from nature. (Notice that James's discourse is characterized by a logic of word association. The "cycle of nature" is mentioned in v. 6, while now in v. 7 nature becomes used as a source for illustrating the writer's convictions concerning speaking and acting.) All creatures, James asserts, can be tamed by human beings, while persons have never succeeded in taming the tongue. Since there is a reference to the creation account in the mention of the image of God in v. 9, this "taming" mentioned in the prior verse probably refers to the "have dominion" reference in the creation account as well. Still, those who are made in God's image can be heard to utter both curses and blessings; we can bless "the Lord and Father" ("Lord" here referring to the first person of the Trinity and not to Christ). The conclusion of this double-talking contradiction is clear: "My brothers and sisters, this ought not to be so" (v. 10). The pericope concludes with a series of rhetorical questions imagistically presenting the overriding issue. No, springs cannot provide both fresh and brackish water nor can one kind of plant yield the fruit of another nor can salt water yield fresh. Just as these images would result in self-contradiction—violating the order of creation—so the tongue of one made in the image of God should not both utter blessing and curse. Such self-contradiction, we are taught, will also be judged with strictness, too.

GOSPEL: MARK 8:27-38

The centerpiece of Mark's Gospel is the account of Jesus and the disciples at Caesarea Philippi. Peter's confession that Jesus is the Messiah, the Christ, is in response to that enduring question, "Who do people say that I am?" (v. 27). That Peter finally was able to see Jesus identity without any double-vision (see 8:22-26) privileges him among his contemporaries. No one in Mark's story of

Jesus fully sees what Mark told us at its beginning, namely, that Jesus is the Christ, the Son of God. Of course, the demons know who Jesus is and a Roman centurion discovers the truth at the cross, but otherwise, Peter's vision is unrivaled in the Gospel. In spite of what others may believe, Jesus is the Messiah, the Promised One of Israel.

Mark immediately suggests, however, that Peter may be double-sighted and double-minded after all. For when he hears the first of three predictions of the passion Jesus will announce in the Gospel, Peter acts to "correct" Jesus' misunderstanding of messiahship. He "took Jesus aside" (v. 32), a gesture usually reserved for those senior in authority to tell those junior in authority how something really is the case and not otherwise. Peter then rebukes Jesus of this notion of a suffering messiah. In response, Jesus immediately turns, peers at his disciples, and rebukes Peter with those damning words, "Get behind me [*opisō mou*], Satan!" (v. 33). Then comes the alternative to getting behind Jesus; it is to come "after me" (*opisō mou*). These are the alternatives presented to Peter and to the other disciples. They will not be "in front," but only follow, and that way is one of suffering, rejection, and death.

The dominical saying that follows the exchange with Peter now presents the paradox of the gospel—those who lose will save and those who attempt to save will lose. The subject of this losing or saving is one's life (*tēn psukēn*), also construed as one's "soul" or "self." Then follows a series of subsidiary statements that serve to intensify the paradox of attempting to save one's life and thereby losing it. Each of these pronouncements begins with "for," including v. 37, which omits the preposition in the NRSV translation. The effect is cumulative and finally reaches to the End. Then and there the paradox will be revealed in all its tragedy, for the Son of Humanity will also be ashamed of all who are ashamed of Christ "when he comes in the glory of his Father with the holy angels" (v. 38).

HOMILETICAL STRATEGIES

Proverbs 1:20-33. The appeal of Woman Wisdom here in the first chapter of Proverbs and the love poem in the last chapter (see the first reading for next Sunday) represent the most narrative literary expressions within the proverbs collection. With this in mind, the most likely strategy for preaching this lection would also be narrative in form. Having said that, however, we are still confronted with a number of narrative approaches to the sermon. One method that commends itself is "contemporizing the story," where the preacher essentially follows the text in sequence but clothes it in present-day apparel (see Eugene Lowry, *How To Preach a Parable: Designs for Narrative Preaching* [Nashville: Abingdon Press, 1989]). Given our own age's lack of wisdom, this project should be both effective and rewarding.

We may begin by locating personified wisdom in the midst of our community. Since wisdom in the Scriptures relates to the theology of creation, her call is to all persons whether or not they are of the household of faith. So we will want to establish this public setting for wisdom's call such that she may be heard both by those within and those outside of the church. Perhaps the setting could be similar to that of the text where she cries out from the public square. Or, given our places of public meeting, could wisdom beckon on the Internet, too, or in the halls of the local high school? The appeal is first directed to "the simple." Recall that the simple are not understood as lacking in I.Q.; rather, they are those who remain adamantly uninformed as to right ways of living. They delight in scoffing and hate knowledge. Now is the occasion for the preacher to get concrete about the ways of the simple. One obvious collection of scoffers, for example, are those who choose to remain addicted to smoking in the face of the wisdom concerning its affects on our health. A strange little truck drives continually through the city streets with a billboard-size rendition of some very cool camels smoking cigarettes. Almost any popular magazine shows us the romance of Marlboro country, where apparently those range riders never get lung cancer or emphysema. We might want to extend the list of ways in which our culture scoffs at wisdom and hates knowledge.

Woman Wisdom's response to all of these deeds and words of the simple is twofold: first, the ways of the simple will lead to calamity. Only now does our culture seem to be hearing Wisdom in her insistence that certain actions will have consequences that are disastrous. A recent report concluded that the total cost in New York City for the consequences of substance abuse—alcohol, tobacco, and drugs—was about twenty billion dollars a year. Perhaps you can invite the congregation to spot similar consequences closer to home, if yours is not a church in New York City. It is important to the movement of the sermon that a distinction is made between the kinds of attitudes and so-called values of the simple (our first section of the plot) and this second section which now deals in consequences. But Wisdom does not stop with just a tally of the calamities brought about by hating knowledge. Finally, when faced with these outcomes, Wisdom will be sought out, but will not be found. There is an end time to Wisdom's patient beckoning. We do not have forever. Eventually, those who reject Wisdom and her ways will have to "eat the fruit of their way."

There is an opposite side of the coin that is more implicit in the Proverbs text but should be held up to the light in our sermon. A promise concludes the pericope related to the wise who listen and live in the ways of wisdom. They will prosper and need not dread disaster. They are characterized by a stance of remaining students of wisdom all their days; they have learned the fear of the Lord. The paradox here is that those who are so self-centered as to ignore wisdom and scoff at understanding wind up in calamity. Those, however, who heed wisdom, fear God, and do not live only to be "sated by their own devices" are those who are promised life in security and abundance. Now it is most likely that all of us who come to hear God's Word this Lord's Day have at least some of the traits of the simple we carry along. Wisdom is right, and we will face those consequences. But Wisdom has not yet given up on us. She calls even in the public places of the church. And the invitation is to love her knowledge, fear the Lord, and be filled with love. The sermon may want to conclude by bringing on home to the church this message of wisdom that leads to life.

James 3:1-12. This pericope from James is a challenge for preachers. Not that its subject matter—the impact for better and for worse of speech within the community of faith—is problematic; to the contrary, the issue abides and is a serious pastoral matter. The challenge, rather, is in the "logic" of the text and its seemingly endless intuitive leaps. At first, we are invited to consider the (mixed) blessing of Christian teachers, then we are shifted to the matter of speaking with three images that follow rapidly upon each other. The text settles down for a bit as the image of the tongue is assessed and the passage concludes with the paradox of good and evil speech proceeding from the same person. There is a logic to all of this, but it is certainly not plottable in the same way that a biblical narrative is, or even, say, a Pauline epistlary sequence. James makes connections here through such literary devices as word associations and he assembles an intuitive tumble of images without taking time to fully explore any of them in-depth. Hence the challenge for the preacher! Of course, the temptation is to extract just a single "gem" from this imagistic quarry and leave the rest of the material for some other time. On the other hand, lurking within the text are several streams of thought with their related image systems that can provide for a homiletic plot that remains both mobile and intentional. What follows is an attempt to track one of these sequences with regard to a series of moves or locations dealing with this critical issues of speech within the body.

1. We are used to controlling things all the time. Look, in our world, success is measured a lot by how well you can exercise control.

For James, the images were of a rudder on a boat or a bridle in the mouth of a horse. Nowadays we talk about controlling fast cars or the flood of stuff on the information superhighway. Maybe we can't control the weather yet, but we try to control almost everything else—gene-engineered crops, low-fat diets, we even try to control violence on TV.

2. Problem is ourselves. James spots it for us—we have a devil of a time controlling our own words. "The tongue is fire," he says, and he is right.

Here's the age-old problem: How do we control what's destructive within ourselves. Look at all the self-help books on the shelves offering us ways to control addictions, codependence, obesity, you name it. It is interesting that few of those titles deal with words that are out of control. But just listen to the raging fires of words in our world today. (Probably the best image here is the radio talk show with the outpouring of words of anger from guests and those who call in.)

3. And look how far the damage goes out. The tongue may be a little member, but it can make the whole body sick.

(Note that this move is ecclesial. It is time to shift our perspective from talk and words in general in the culture to their use or misuse within the church.) Ever hear of "triangulation"? It is a way that words can spread evil like a forest fire throughout a church. All you do is follow one simple rule; Never talk directly to anyone about any problem between you. So we go and tell person #2 about our problem and she tells person #3 and he tells person #4. Soon we have spread our anger or anxiety enough that the stress inside feels better. But look at the damage out there. Now everyone is stressed and angry. And through all these triangle paths, our words never get things resolved. Result: the congregation catches the "triangulation flu" and it stays sick.

4. "Bless the Lord," is the advice. But be consistent and bless each other, too!

But thanks be to God, we can use our words for good—we can bless the Lord our God. Remember how we began our worship, how we sang (here we can invite the congregation to reflect on the hymn of praise at the opening of the liturgy)? From the beginning of creation, God intended this of all of us human creatures, that we use our mouths to declare the praise of our maker. And do you know what else, too? There at the beginning, too, was God's purpose that we bless each other, bless all creation with our words of healing and love. (How do we image this positive move about words that bless and heal? What about the scene in *Jurassic Park* when a huge dinosaur sneezes and the boy shouts out, "God bless you!"?)

5. Speak "benedictions," "good words," and the signs that a people are doing good. Speaking good bears fruit in our actions.

Here, the focus is on the fruits of "good works" once more. More particularly, the concluding single meaning here deals with the actions that issue forth from a community whose speech reflects the Gospel. Ever notice how certain people have the virtue of always saying something good about other folks? Even when it is clear that it would be easier to say a word or ridicule or condemnation? And the sisters and brother who spread those "benedictions" around, look at how they live. They are endless fresh fountains of caring and love. (Here we must image such persons. Perhaps an illustration, a story, could be employed. However, it may be best to keep this images system as close as possible to the lived experience of the assembly. Have they known a pastor whose words and actions reflected this continuum from benediction to good works? Perhaps a series of examples might be provided for the hearers to consider and celebrate.)

Mark 8:27-38. The passage that is widely known as "Peter's confession" also needs to be titled, "Peter's rebuke." That is, the two coordinates of the pericope are first Peter's achievement with reference to Jesus' question, "But who do you say that I am?" Second, there is a lack of knowledge shown by Peter when he takes Jesus aside and rebukes him for the passion prediction. Not only is Jesus' true identity and vocation at stake here; so are the identity and vocation of anyone who follows Jesus as well. One approach to a homiletic strategy could be to follow a trajectory beginning with the Caesarea Philippi location—a place of Gentile religious "pluralism" without rival in first-century Palestine. We could then follow Peter's responses—and our own—to Jesus' question addressed to every disciple. The "scenes" of this narrative homiletic plot, then, would run as follows:

1. Jesus asks his disciples the big question: "Who do you say that I am?" Odd, though, that he didn't pick a place more conducive to spiritual reflection, like beside the Sea of Galilee. No, he takes the Twelve up to Caesarea Philippi, a place named "Philip is Caesar" ("Lord"). Not only that, the place used to be called "Pantown" in honor of the Greek God Pan before the Romans came. In fact, Jesus could have popped the question beneath the cliff way next to the town where numerous niches were carved for the statues of the many Greek deities, now in a place named "Philip is Lord." In the most "pluralistic" and therefore unholy place imaginable to a good Jew, Jesus asks the question. (Now it is up to the preacher to provide the analogies in our own context for the question. Probably Jesus does not decide to pop the question to us most forcefully when we are sitting at a campfire at church camp beside the lake under the stars. But for the hearers on this Sunday, where and when would Jesus ask us about himself?)

2. In spite of the distractions of this religious marketplace, Peter does get it right. "Messiah," he blurts out. "You are the Christ." Peter is no doubt looking back to the south, on past Galilee to Jerusalem. (Caesarea Philippi is way up north above Galilee.) Jerusalem—that is where Peter's confession will be enacted in public and in glory. Just imagine, Jesus entering his own city in procession with palms and shouts of acclamation. Here comes royal David's Son into David's city. Yes, for Peter, the correction of other people's mistaken notions of Jesus will happen in the holy city. (We may want to image this Peter's perception from some of the popular hymns or art that reflect Peter's view. The important function of this scene is to establish the true identity of Jesus as the Messiah. What is mistaken about Peter's understanding—and possibly ours as well—is its triumphalism.)

3. Now comes the teaching from Jesus that disrupts Peter's expectations. Jesus, too, may be looking south from Caesarea Philippi, past Galilee, and on to Jerusalem. But what he sees there is "great suffering," rejection by the religious authorities, and death. Oh, he adds that part about "and after three days rise again," but that does not figure into the view held by Peter since it does not

allow for suffering. Each of the three passion predictions in Mark is located alongside a startling opposition. Here, in the first announcement of the destiny of the Son of Humanity, the alignment is "Messiah" and "great suffering." Each element is now brought into a new unity—the Messiah will suffer and be killed. How shall we image this in the sermon? (Notice that if we chose a hymn text as an illustration of the previous scene in the sermon plot, we would not want to repeat such usage in this next scene with another hymn text. The two scenes would tend to merge into a confused blending in the congregational hearing.) Perhaps one could make a reference to the film *Jesus of Montreal*, in which even an actor playing Jesus in a passion play winds up so identified with Christ that he, too, comes to suffer and die.

4. Now is the scene of the dual rebukes. We need not develop Peter's response to Jesus' words into a full scene, although that strategy is an option if real resistance to Christ's suffering is a pastoral issue for the preacher to address. Still, we probably will need to glance at Peter's words and actions, his condescending "taking aside" of Jesus. Images come easily to mind of analogies in the lived experience of the congregation of this attitude in action. The response of Jesus, with its rebuke and sting of the label, "Satan," may want to have at least "equal time" here. If Peter's words imply a senior to a junior status, Jesus' words in return speak of stark opposition. Perhaps an image system here that lists ways in which the world and the church try to delete the cross from Christian experience and theology could be provided, all ending in the tagline, "And Jesus responds to Peter and to us, 'get behind me, get behind me, Satan.'" One such image could be "new age" notions of spirituality that suggest that all suffering is avoidable, or illusory.

5. Of course, the other option is to get behind Jesus as his disciples. He will not tolerate us up "in front" determining the way for ourselves. We will either be told to get behind him in a rebuke or hear his gentle invitation to follow him. Either way, Christ will lead the way to Jerusalem, to the cross, and also lead the way from death to resurrection. Ours is to follow faithfully and in great hope that through the way of suffering comes healing and through death comes eternal life. Perhaps here the preacher may want to point to ways of following Jesus within the parish and in the community. This is the time in the sermon to point to positive examples of discipleship and to conclude with Jesus' invitation to "Follow me."

Eighteenth Sunday after Pentecost
Twenty-Fifth Sunday in Ordinary Time
Proper 20

Lectionary	First Lesson	Psalm	Second Lesson	Gospel
Revised Common	Prov. 31:10-31 *or* Wis. 1:16—2:1, 12-22 *or* Jer. 11:18-20	Psalm 1 *or* 54	James 3:13—4:3, 7-8a	Mark 9:30-37
Episcopal (BCP)	Wis. 1:16—2:1, (6-11), 12-22	Psalm 54	James 3:16—4:6	Mark 9:30-37
Roman Catholic	Wis. 2:12, 17-20	Ps. 54:3-8	James 3:16—4:3	Mark 9:30-37
Lutheran (LBW)	Jer. 11:18-20	Ps. 54:1-4, 6-7a	James 3:16—4:6	Mark 9:30-37

FIRST LESSON: PROVERBS 31:10-31

The hymn to a good wife in 31:10-31 can be read as a continuation of this advice given to "King Lemuel that his mother taught him," beginning at 31:1. On the other hand, the pericope (31:10-31) serves as an epilogue to the entire Book of Proverbs and may therefore have a source independent of the Lemuel tradition. The distinctiveness of the pericope is heightened by its literary form, being an acrostic poem with each verse beginning with the next letter of the Hebrew alphabet. Moreover, the structure of the poem embodies a chiastic form with v. 23 at the center of the chiasmus. (Notice, for example, the parallels in the content of vv. 22 and 24, 21 and 25, and so forth.) That the central text of the chiasmus addresses the place of honor of the husband of such a good wife suggests that the audience of the pericope was intended to be that of young men. Their need, therefore, was both a good wife, honor within the community, and wisdom. The poem encompasses all three of these necessities.

The poem begins with the rhetorical question of finding such a capable wife. It is interesting that the root Hebrew word translated "capable" more generally means "strength," often connoting strength in its military expression. (Perhaps the translators should have made this connotation more explicit by giving "mission capable" as the rendering of *hayil*!) Such a woman is to be highly valued as a wife, a conclusion also appearing in the last two verses of the text. Moving one further step in toward the central affirmation of the chiasmus in v. 23, we notice an attention given to husband and family and 31:11-12 and 28. A husband may trust such a good wife within his "heart," also meaning his inmost self. He is blessed both in this inward dimension and outwardly as well—there will be "no lack of grain" (v. 11). Both her children and her husband will praise her and accord her honor (v. 28). The next section of the chiastic structure deals with the good wife's domestic industry and social commerce. We are given to see a woman skilled in varied gifts such as spinning and weaving and bartering and buying and selling. There is a constancy to her application of these virtues;

moreover, she does not "eat the bread of idleness" (v. 27). These verse parallels do not establish the stereotyped view that "a woman's place is in the home." Rather, the good wife is equally diligent and skilled in domestic matters and in those of the commercial arena, ensuring that "her merchandise is profitable" (v. 18). Whether concerned with the buying of a field or the caring for her household, the good wife is "mission capable" in all respects.

Notable within these parallel sections of the poem is attention to the good wife's strength and dignity on the one hand and her piety before the Lord on the other. She is clothed with strength (v. 25) as she thereby clothes both her family (vv. 21-22) and also the poor (v. 20)! Woven within the same verses as the image system of clothing is the metaphor of "hands." Again serving to link her domestic activity with that of her pious caring for others beyond the family, her hands both "hold the spindle" as well as reach out to the poor. Reflecting the care shown to family and the needy, she is a woman of wisdom and "the teaching of kindness is on her tongue" (v. 26). The Hebrew for "kindness" here is *hesed*, a root word interpreted elsewhere as "devotion" and in the prophetic literature as "steadfast love." As a woman of wisdom, "mission-capable" in her strength and piety, the compilers of this collection give flesh and bones to the image of Wisdom who calls out for the wise in the opening chapter of the collection. Now we discover her identity and all young men who seek a wife and wisdom are urged with all urgency to look for her and to become one with her.

SECOND LESSON: JAMES 3:13—4:8

Once more, James picks up a topic first mentioned earlier in the epistle and now explores it more deeply. In the section, 3:13-18, that issue is wisdom and attitudes and actions which derive from it and stand in opposition to it. In v. 13, wisdom is affirmed as that gift which, while residing within a person, shows forth in a "good life," by good works. Retaining the inner/outer motif, the writer now shifts attention along the spectrum from true wisdom to that which is demonic. In a middle ground lies the inner states of persons whose hearts are filled with "bitter envy and selfish ambition" (v. 14). The outer manifestation of this inner condition is indicated as boastfulness and repudiation of the truth (*pseudesthe kata tes aletheias*, lit., "false to the truth"). At the opposite end of the spectrum from true wisdom is not really another kind of wisdom, but a sort of "unwisdom" that is earthly and devilish rather than "from above" (v. 17). The outward manifestations of this unwisdom are not immediately mentioned, but will be noted extensively in the next section of the pericope. What are noted with some expansiveness in vv. 17-18 are the virtues that derive from that real wisdom "from above" (*anothen*). Once more, "partiality" or discrimination is picked for mention as counter to wisdom come from God.

The following material (4:1-8) is considerably less organized at first glance than is the previous section on wisdom. Initially, the writer of the epistle is drawing on a logic that reverses what was assumed in the discussion about speaking. Here, the alternatives are between inner conditions and outward behavior. Hence, outward contentiousness, these "conflicts and disputes" (v. 1), originate within those who are at war within themselves. There is a selfish desire which is not immediately fulfilled and the reaction is behavior that is evil. "Committing murder" has long been the object of consideration by interpreters of the letter. Does James mean to say that the assembly has been engaged in murder in its life together? Or does the writer once more take the most extreme hypothetical for the readers to imagine? Either way, James wants to impress on those readers that their inner conditions will necessarily manifest themselves in outer behavior, for better or for worse. Let the inner condition become that of a devilish kind of unwisdom, and even murder can result!

That latter portion of the section comprising 4:1-8 now shifts the dichotomy from inner/outer to that of the life in community/life in the world. Here there can be no "both/and" kind of attitude; to become friends with the world is to become "an enemy of God" (v. 5). The dichotomy is spelled out now with regard to inner conditions and outer manifestations. Those of the world are proud, double-minded, and of the devil, while those of the Spirit show humility, purity, and grace. The admonition then follows with force: "Resist the devil." What is good news is the added grace note, "and he will flee from you" (v. 7). Just as in the baptismal liturgy, after the renunciation of Satan, there comes the gift of the Spirit. Here, too, with the devil now fled from sight, God will draw near in the gift of wisdom from above and the Spirit who will dwell within us.

GOSPEL: MARK 9:30-37

It continues to be the case that Jesus privileges the Twelve with an "insiders" teaching, explaining "everything in private to his disciples" (4:34). Once before, immediately following Peter's confession and rebuke, the disciples were "told openly" of the necessity for the Son of Humanity to suffer and die, and only then be raised from the dead. Now, passing once more through Galilee, Jesus privileges the disciples with a second prophecy of betrayal, death, and after three days, the rising of the Son of Humanity. The second passion prediction is both less extensive in description than the first—perhaps more ancient?—and now adds the word *betrayal*, connoting a solidarity with the deaths of Israel's prophets who also were "betrayed." The implication in chap. 4 of the insider/outsider motif was that while the crowds might not understand everything spoken in parables, the disciples would know the secrets of the kingdom taught privately by Jesus. But now, speaking openly to them about his death, Jesus once more finds the response to be both a lack of understanding and a hardness of heart. The narrator informs us of the lack of understanding shared by the disciples who were strangely "afraid to ask him" (v. 32). We learn of the continuing hardness of their hearts as they argue with each other over who was the greatest! The scene parallels that of 8:14-21 in the interplays of the disciples' lack of understanding and Jesus' understanding of their complaints and dissension. Of course, the absence of understanding is not simply a matter of mental grasp, but of a failure of moral and spiritual imagination.

Once more adopting the role of the Teacher, or simply out of weariness, Jesus now sits down and yet again speaks openly to the Twelve. They are told of the profound reversal that is at the hearts of the secrets of the reign of God—first-seekers must become last-seekers, adding, "and the servant (*diakonos*) of all" (v. 35). All talk of greatness, Jesus teaches, is out of place among disciples, especially now that they are on the way to the cross with their Lord. Of course, the disciples will not understand this either, and yet again misunderstanding will result in anger and division among them (see 10:35-45). There is a persistent relationship between this lack of understanding of Jesus' vocation and identity by his followers and the incapacity of those followers to live together in love and peace. The two follow one another predictably, and tragically as well.

Jesus now invites the Twelve to see and thereby understand; he takes a child up in his arms and speaks of welcome. This teacher has shamed himself through this act, become "last of all" by holding an inconsequential child. To welcome such a child, Jesus announces, is to welcome him, and the one who sent him as well. Of course, to do such a thing is of necessity to select the place occupied by servants, the one called "last of all." The image of Jesus holding the child and speaking of hospitality is profoundly striking and ironic for those who have eyes to see. The world will kill the One betrayed into their hands, extending no hospitality whatsoever to the Son of Humanity. And the disciples have no understanding and fight with each other about greatness. There is hope in all this, however. Jesus did add that he will rise again, and promises great privilege to any servants of his who extend hospitality to the child and childlike in faith. They will be blessed to find they have welcomed their Lord and their God.

HOMILETICAL STRATEGIES

Proverbs 31:10-31. Two strategies for preaching the pericope suggest themselves, according to the pastoral and liturgical context. Our text, the hymn to the good wife, portrays a "wonder-working woman" whose sweep of competencies range from the domestic to the mercantile. Moreover, she shows compassion toward the poor, caring for them along with her family. The first strategy, then, would be that of locating a series of narratives of contemporary women and women of the tradition who exemplify aspects of the good wife's capabilities. Some of these stories may be known to the hearers while others may be of women in other locales or from other biblical times and church history. The method would involve the alignment of one of these exemplary stories next to one element in the hymn. For example, in some western and midwestern locations, stories persist of some notable pioneer woman who demonstrated the kinds of strengths tallied in vv. 12-17. A brief telling of her story would therefore be aligned with that opening portion of the Proverbs text. Others stories, then, would follow, also aligned with further descriptions of the capable wife. In each case, the concluding element in the illustrative story could be a repeating of the biblical text as a tagline.

A second strategy for preaching Prov. 31:10-31 takes a different approach. Given that the stated purpose of the text is the instruction of young men regarding their choices in marriage, the text almost of necessity points to virtues necessary for life in a covenant marriage and for life in covenant in a church family. It is not inappropriate, therefore, to invite the congregation to hear what capabilities they need to possess, within their own households and within the church household. And while we probably cannot devote attention to every one of the competencies attributed to the capable wife in the text, we can choose a sequence that will both flow and speak pastorally to the hearers. We would do well in arranging the sequence of competencies with one of those two image systems in mind—the image of being "clothed" or of extending the "hand." The former image, then, could focus the hearers first on their roles in providing for clothing for their own family or church family. Perhaps a team of capable sewers have turned from making clothes for their family and produced a lovely set of new robes for the acolytes. Or maybe the "quilters," a wonderful gathering of older women in the parish, have just made a striking altar hanging and are now working on infant-size quilts for a shelter for battered women. (You get the idea. The preacher would identify particular competencies of the capable women in the pericope, expand on that depiction in the text, and then point to examples of those competencies being lived out in the lives of families within the church and within the church family.)

James 3:13—4:3, 7-8a. The argument in our reading from James presents us with several renditions of ways of life that are of God or of the devil. Along the way, the writer of the epistle develops a notion of wisdom fully in harmony with the wisdom tradition of the Hebrew Scripture. And the author also shows an interest, in accord with that wisdom tradition, with both the outer actions of a person and the inner conditions that give birth to those actions. James invites the reader to focus or involve the following sequence of oppositions:

Wisdom from above	Wisdom that is earthly
Good fruits of gentleness, mercy, impartiality, peace	Bad fruits of conflicts, discrimination, disorder, wickedness, etc.
Inner conditions of purity and nearness to God	Inner conditions of selfishness, unbridled cravings, and ungodly envy
Peacefulness in the world and within the heart	"Murder" in the world and conflict with the heart

As we consider the question of a strategy for preaching these oppositions within the pericope, one sequence commends itself by focusing first on praxis, on behavior, and then exploring the condition underlying those outcomes. The sermonic plot, then, could begin by inviting the congregation to look at the "bad fruits" of earthly wisdom, then explore the underlying negative spiritual states that give rise to those conditions. The sermon could next move to an examination of the actions of the wise that would then lead to an exploratory angiogram into the hearts of the godly. The sequence in brief, to be expanded through analysis and imagery, involves the following plot:

> The "bad fruits" of the unwise→the internal conditions of ungodliness→
> the "good fruits" of the wise→the internal conditions of the godly.

Because the epistle deals with both ecclesial and worldly aspects of the wise/unwise dichotomy, the preacher will need to take some care in balancing the two. Clearly James sees the same dynamics for good and for evil at work in church and society, including even "murder in the cathedral"! What we want to avoid is a sermon that rearranges the oppositions in the text in order that, for example, we portray all the negativity as "out there in the world" and all things bright and beautiful "in here in the church." Just as distorting would be an approach that reversed the ideological picture to now equate church as bad and world as good. Nevertheless, it is clear that James does see the good fruits of the wise as abounding in those who draw near to God. The church, therefore, should be a place, not of "murder" (literal or otherwise), but of peace and purity. One other caution here. In any sermon in which a dialectic ethical structure organizes the plot, there is usually no shortage of examples of the negative expressions in outer behavior and inner conditions of the heart. The challenge in preaching this kind of text is in providing even more brilliant and concrete examples of wisdom's fruits and wisdom's inner godliness. Otherwise, our hearers go away more depressed than encouraged; the intent of the epistle is thwarted as well.

Mark 9:30-37. The Gospel lection is a striking story that centers on Jesus' second passion prediction in Mark. In that story, there are two pronouncements by Jesus to the disciples—and to the readers/hearers. First, there is the passion prediction itself and, second, the dominical statement concerning hospitality to the child that concludes the pericope. However, Mark the narrator also provides important information to us concerning the disciples: first, that they did not understand Jesus' words about his death; second, that they were silent because they were afraid; and last, that they had argued over greatness among themselves. The fact that, as Mark begins, Jesus did not want anyone to know of his teaching to the disciples underscores the importance of those of us who are the hearers/readers. We are let in on the privileged teaching along with the Twelve!

There is an elegant interplay in the story related to Mark's use of the image of the child. The clear message to be drawn from Mark's information to us about the disciples—their lack of understanding, their fear and silence, and their argument over greatness—is that they are a bunch of overgrown children.

You can almost hear these kinds of conversations going on out in the elementary school playground. Once we have reached this conclusion, and are therefore ready to reject those twelve "kids" out of hand, Jesus takes up a child in his arms and speaks to us of hospitality! For those of us who have ears to hear, the "fit" with our own situation may be tight in the extreme. Here is where the preacher may now serve the Word. Taking a strategy that "runs the story," we may invite our listeners in on the journey Mark recounts and hear with the Twelve Jesus' own words about his suffering and death. We will want to pause at this passion prediction for a bit, to allow the congregation to "remember forward" to the events at the cross. For parishes in which Palm/Passion Sunday involved both the service of the palms and the narrative of the passion drama, we may recall with our hearers the way our "hosannas" on that Sunday turned to solemn grief as we listened to the story and sang "Wondrous Love" (or whatever passion hymn was sung). It is important in this sermon, which follows the sequence of Mark's story, that the hearers live into Jesus' cross-shaped words. Only with such a depth of insight will the response of the disciples become sufficiently ironic that Mark will be able to do with us what he intends. (*See my Narrative & Imagination*, chap. 4, for a discussion of the role of irony in interpretation and preaching.)

Narrative irony involves a rather "hidden" conversation between the narrator and the reader. In this case, Mark depicts these childish disciples with their arguments and fearful silence and lack of understanding. These behaviors and inner conditions now are described for the congregation and the preacher may rightfully have all of us get quite upset with those "kids." Our anger is appropriate and intended by the irony Mark employs. Perhaps our stance, our point of view shaped by the preacher, is that of parents wearied by these children of ours. Our point of view, then, is in solidarity with that of Jesus who must also be profoundly wearied. The point of view held by the congregation may then be disrupted by the preacher—will of necessity *need* to be disrupted. We are also like the Twelve in so many ways! As preachers, it will be our task to invite our hearers to see the distance between ourselves and the Twelve slip away. Finally, any sense of distance will collapse entirely. The point of view has drastically shifted for the assembly. We are all like that bunch of kids, fearful and silent, lacking understanding, and posturing for greatness. It is at this point that Jesus sits down. (He will remain standing until that place in the sermon where the irony of our own situation has been exposed.) Now, he takes that child, takes all of us kids, and speaks of welcome. Clearly, we are to welcome those who come as a child to the reign of God. But the other side of the coin is that we have been welcomed, even as petulant and fearful as we are. According to the pastoral situation, the sermon will want to conclude either with the focus on our extending that hospitality to others or, perhaps the primary interest of the pericope, on seeing even ourselves as welcomed by our Lord.

Nineteenth Sunday after Pentecost
Twenty-Sixth Sunday in Ordinary Time
Proper 21

Lectionary	First Lesson	Psalm	Second Lesson	Gospel
Revised Common	Est. 7:1-6, 9-10; 9: 20-22 or Num. 11: 4-6, 10-16, 24-29	Psalm 124 or Ps. 19:7-14	James 5:13-20	Mark 9:38-50
Episcopal (BCP)	Num. 11:4-6, 10-16, 24-29	Ps. 19 or 19:7-14	James 4:7-12 (13— 5:6)	Mark 9:38-43, 45, 47-48
Roman Catholic	Num. 11:25-29	Ps. 19:8-20, 12-14	James 5:1-6	Mark 9:38-43, 45, 47-48
Lutheran (LBW)	Num. 11: 4-6, 10-16, 24-29	Ps. 135:1-7, 13-14	James 4:7-12 (13— 5:6)	Mark 9:38-50

FIRST LESSON: ESTHER 7:1-6, 9-10; 9:20-22

The story of Esther is set in imperial Persia, at the time of the rule of king Ahasuerus. At the outset, we learn that the king is a lover of banquets—the opening feast lasting one hundred and eighty days!—and that in the royal court there was also a fondness for position, for ceremony, and for the laws of the land. Following the first and most extensive feast of the story, a lesser feast of only seven days duration is given for the people of Susa, the seat of the throne; Ahasuerus's queen, Vashti, also gives a banquet for all of the women. It was on the seventh and last day of this lesser feast that the king summons his queen in order to show off her beauty to the people and the officials. By the seventh day the king "was merry with wine" (1:10). Vashti, however, refuses to be shown off, and is summarily dismissed as queen by Ahasuerus. With the throne vacant, the king begins a search among the virgins of the land for a new queen. The process is extended, complex, and, ultimately, fruitful (see 2:1-18). The adopted daughter of Mordecai, a Jewish woman named Esther, wins the king's favor and is crowned queen. Of course, there is a banquet!

Now the plot thickens as a certain Haman is promoted by the king to the status above that of every other official in the realm. And while every lesser official then bows down before Haman, Mordecai the Jew refuses. Discovering that the reason for this insubordination was Mordecai's Jewish faith, Haman plots a pogrom to exterminate all of the Jews in the kingdom. He enacts a lot (*pur*) to determine the month and day of the murderous deed and convinces the king of the necessity of eliminating a people who do not keep the king's laws. Accordingly, detailed instructions are sent out to every official in every province "to destroy, to kill, and to annihilate all Jews" (3:13). Haman and the king then seal the plan with feasting and drinking.

The plot thus far has been propelled by these feasts with their endless drinking—first indicating the manner in which Esther becomes queen and then settling the plan for the destruction of all the Jews in the empire. Now a new sequence of banquets reverse the fortunes of Haman and the Jews, this time given by Queen Esther. The first of these (5:1-8) depicts the king's deepened favor for his queen, offering her one half of his kingdom, or the granting of any petition she may make. Esther petitions that the king and Haman come the next day to, of course, another banquet. Here our pericope picks up the plot.

The reading begins by setting the stage for this second of Esther's banquets. "So the king and Haman went in to feast with Queen Esther" (7:1). We hardly need to reflect on the fact that there seem to be more banquets in the story of Esther than in the rest of the narratives of the Hebrew Scriptures combined! This feast, however, is crucial. The king once more asks for Esther's petition and she responds by petitioning for her life and the lives of her people to be spared. In v. 4, Esther recounts, word for word, the treacherous directive by Haman to all the officials of the empire. When the king asks the identity of the one who presumed to do this, Esther reveals Haman as "foe and enemy" (v. 6). The reversal is swift in coming and Haman's status sinks rapidly before the king; the very gallows he had erected to hang Mordecai becomes his own. "Then the anger of the king abated" (v. 10).

In an epilogue to the story, Mordecai corresponds to all the Jews wherever in the provinces of King Ahasuerus, placing upon them the obligation to feast for the two days following the now voided date of their executions. In a parody of the Persian officialdom, Mordecai engages in this preparation for festivity with the same kind of officiousness that Haman had employed to attempt the awful pogrom. And, of course, the command is to feast and be glad. In fact, there have been all kinds of reasons for feasting in the story, along with the reason of "no reason at all." But Esther's two banquets and the feasts of Purim have this in common—the reason for the feast is the deliverance of God's people.

SECOND LESSON: JAMES 5:13-20

The pericope opens with a rhetorical system designed for instruction. This "Are any . . . ? They should . . ." series deals with those in the community who are suffering ("They should pray"); who are cheerful ("they should sing songs of praise"); or who are sick ("they should call for the elders"). Only the last of these conditions is expanded upon in vv. 14 and 15. Those who are called by the sick are "elders of the church" (*presbuterous tēs ekklēsias*). James typically employs *sunagōgē* for the community; although *ekklēsias* is unique to this reference, it is the usual term for the church elsewhere in the New Testament. The elders of the church first are to pray over the sick persons they visit, then anointing them with oil "in the name of the Lord" (v. 14). The writer does not suggest innovation here; the implication is clearly that the office and ministries of the presbyter are ongoing realities within the community.

Verse 15 serves both to expand on the role of prayer for the sick as well as generalize the discussion. The sick will be saved (*sōsei*) through prayer and will be raised up (*egerei*) by the Lord. Moreover, through prayer, "anyone who has committed sins will be forgiven" (v. 15). What is not assumed here is that the sin in question has caused any specific illness within the community. Certainly there is a relationship between healing and forgiveness—elaborated in the next verse—but there is no implication here that all illness originates from sin. James now locates the ministries dealing with sin more clearly within an ecclesial context. The confession of sin is to be "to one another," as, in fact, all prayer should be. Members of the community are to be praying for each other, confessing to each other, and forgiving each other. Healing and health thereby grace the community as well as the individual member.

Within the *ekklēsia*, the ministries of prayer and healing are particularly efficacious with respect to the righteous, whose prayers are "powerful and effective" (v. 16). Full, active prayer is a significant charism within the church. Implied in this affirmation is an invitation to all within the community to a life of deeper prayer, especially prayer for one another. Somewhat oddly, Elijah is singled out as exemplary of this kind of active praying. Desiring drought, Elijah "prayed fervently" and it came to pass as did the end of the drought, again through fervent prayer. James's convictions here are conveyed through use of the Elijah figure—prayer is critical to healing, to forgiveness, and even to the healing of nature (as through prayer "the heaven gave rain and the earth yielded its harvest.")

The final section of the pericope shifts its attention to those who are wandering from the truth and from the community. The goal of all the faithful should be the retrieval of such wanderers from sin and for the community. Being brought back, the wanderer's sins are covered and the sinner's soul is saved from death. Envisioned here is a community fervent in prayer for each other, prayers that are for healing and forgiveness, and for the reconciliation of any who wander into sin.

GOSPEL: MARK 9:38-50

The coordinates within the material following Jesus' second prediction of the passion (9:33ff.) have proved to be those of the identity of Jesus along with his vocation, the nature of hospitality within the community, and the image of the child, both literally and figuratively as a person of new faith in Christ. The lection for this Sunday opens with the disciples now complaining to Jesus that they have spotted someone casting out demons and have tried to stop him. Obviously the issue of hospitality is once more on the table, but so is the question of the identity and authority of Jesus. This itinerant exorcist was casting out demons—apparently an effective ministry—in the name of Jesus, yet the disciples move to quash this ministry because "he was not following us." The logic here appears to be that hospitality is to be extended to those who follow the disciples, in spite of the fact that Jesus linked servanthood and hospitality so intimately in the prior conversation. Moreover, the readers may detect the irony in this complaint by the disciples that the exorcist was not "following

us"; the narrative since the first passion prediction in 8:31 has largely concerned itself with the implications of following Jesus. The complaint by the
Twelve reveals to Jesus and to the readers that the disciples have not grasped
that they are called to follow Jesus and extend hospitality to those "little ones."
Their reference to an exorcist who is not following them discloses further lack
of understanding of their own vocation and of that of Jesus as well.

Mark now extends the hospitality reference in v. 37 with two additional
"whoever" statements (9:41, 42). The first of these statements reverses the point
of view persistently held by the disciples. Once more, they are invited to imagine themselves the potential recipients of hospitality extended by others, this
time in the form of a cup of water. There is an interesting interplay between this
dominical saying and that earlier complaint of the disciples about the exorcist.
The latter was casting out demons "in your name," while those who will not
lose the reward in v. 41 are precisely those who welcome disciples because they
"bear the name of Christ." The second "whoever" statement once more shifts
point of view. Now, Jesus addresses the disciples with an injunction about the
perils of not extending hospitality to "these little ones." The prospects are
indeed gloomy for such ungrateful servants! What follows, then, are a series of
admonitions cast in stark detail that weigh the merits of trying to save oneself
and thereby losing oneself. In every case, even self-mutilation is far better than
the consequences of causing one of these little ones to stumble.

The pericope closes with the words of Jesus concerning the image of salt in
relation to discipleship. To be a salty disciple is to follow Jesus, the Messiah,
and to extend hospitality, especially to "these little ones" who are young in
faith. Since we have seen the disciples repeatedly fall into dissension with
each other following their misunderstanding of what Jesus had taught them,
the conclusion here is clear. Salty Christians are also to "be at peace with one
another" (v. 49). The conditions that make for a community of exclusion that is
at war within itself are by now very clear. At the heart of the matter is the per-
sisting question of Jesus' identity and of the role of the disciples to follow him,
welcoming the children in faith, and joining with a diverse group of others
who have also decided to follow Jesus.

HOMILETICAL STRATEGIES

Esther 7:1-6, 9-10; 9:20-22. The story of Esther practically insists that it be
preached as a story. In fact, after hearing the wonderful tale, a discursive
exploration of some of the narrative's "points" would seem wildly out of
place. Some may raise the question of how the story figures into the church's
homiletic canon; the specifically "Christian" application of this oriental tale
does seem problematic. Still, to the extent that we Christians are through our
baptism all "adopted Jews," it is certainly sufficient for us to tell and hear the
Esther story in solidarity with the rest of Israel! This is not to say that the story
does not evoke issues of contemporary application, however. Perhaps we best
spot those analogies as we trace the four decisive feasts of the tale.

Feast 1: Esther is chosen as queen. The protocols here are as complex and convoluted as those pertaining to all the other aspects of royal life among the Medes and the Persians. Only the "Miss America" pageant rivals the ceremonies and ordered procedures of King Ahasueras! Interesting items are disclosed, though, within the description of the search for a queen—Jews are present within the kingdom (remaining there from the time of the exile) and Mordecai, among them, has some status in the king's citadel, and also has an adopted cousin, Esther. The need for her adoption is perhaps located in the awful dislocation and carnage of the exile itself, although that is only speculation, speculation certainly evoked by the story itself. Esther becomes the winner of this coerced beauty pageant, but in a surprising turn, the king falls in love with her, preferring her to all the other women of his harem. Esther becomes his queen. There is, of course, a banquet. The preacher might observe in passing how tragedy lies in the background of the story—the exile—and how love managed to blossom even in the midst of this exploitative process of the search for a queen.

Feast 2: The feast, or really a drinking session, is the finale to the plot development by which Haman is advanced to a position superior to every other official under the king. The consequence of the elevation is that all must bow before Haman, and all do bow, except, . . . yes, Mordecai the Jew. In a rage, Haman contrives to kill all the Jews of the kingdom, convinces the king of the needed action, and sets the date for the execution of the progrom by the throw of the lot. (Esther, we recall, has not informed the king that she is a Jew.) The feast—or drinking session—at the end of this sequence of treachery and evil seals the deal. And while they quaff the king's wine, "the city of Susa was thrown into confusion." The preacher here might now point to contemporary examples of similar abuses of power, especially where the innocent learn of their impending suffering. The Holocaust immediately looms with its six million horrid images—it has now become the intratext of the story of Esther for all of the covenant people. On a much less massive scale, other "sealed deal" kinds of feasting of those with power may come to mind.

Feast 3: Esther's banquet. The queen had options she did not take. She could have ridden out the purge by herself (Ahasuerus does not know she is a Jew). Or she could have maneuvered to save only her uncle Mordecai, entreating a special dispensation by the king. Instead, she uses the favorite device of the king as the occasion to thwart Haman entirely—a feast. The plan is not without risk to Esther; she is a Jew and the time for their destruction is growing near. Still, it is not until day two of the feast that Esther makes her move. On the feast's first day, she goes through all the motions of a queen enjoying a banquet given for her king! Then, in response to the king's offer to Esther of anything (she can petition for half of his kingdom) she intercedes for herself and her people. In so doing, Haman's plot is uncovered and he is ruined. The gallows Haman erected for Mordecai becomes his own instrument of execution. Mordecai is now granted the king's ring once worn by the traitor Haman—all of this in the context of Esther's banquet. The preacher may want to invite the congregation to spot some of the reversals that have occurred in feast number three, involving the images of gallows and ring. We may also invite the hearers to become more capable at spotting such ironic reversals in our contemporary situations as well. (One bishop known for his attacks on alcohol and homosexuality died of AIDS. It was learned that he led two lives, one a hidden life in the gay bars of Houston.)

Feast 4: Now comes the communal feast. All of the Jews in the vast kingdom are to feast on the two days following the date that was to have been their execution. We notice that the festival is commanded, an interesting turn on all of the other laws of the Medes and the Persians. What is now ordered is a feast of liberation and deliverance. We may observe that another feast is commanded of us, also of liberation. And as we are preparing to offer the gifts of bread and wine for this feast, we do well to remember Esther and thank God for her wisdom and her courage. We might also make a special point this year to send greetings to our Jewish sisters and brothers when they gather to celebrate the feast of Purim at a synagogue nearby.

James 5:13-20. The series of instructions in the lection deal with those within the community of faith who suffer and are sick, who need forgiveness, and those who are cheerful. To deal with this text homiletically is most probably also to make a liturgical decision in favor of a service of prayer and anointing for the sick as a response to the Word. Since the instructions are straightforward, the sermon may begin with the pastoral issue of resistance to sharing our suffering with the church. The pericope stands in strong opposition to any "individualistic" notions of sickness and suffering; these conditions are to be shared with the community in order that the ministry of prayer and of healing may occur. A "Lowry Loop" type of homiletic plot may set up this barrier to prayer and healing and thereby invite the members of the church to a fuller sharing of their needs with each other.

1. The problem: We often do not share with each other when we are sick. Over and over, the congregation hears about someone who has been in the hospital after they are discharged. The response from that sister or brother is often, "Well, I didn't want to bother anyone." Our response—probably we are now bothered!

2. Analysis: But why in the world wouldn't we want to share our sufferings with the community? They are our family! Maybe for some the issue is that old myth of self-sufficiency. We should be able to take care of ourselves, not be "a burden" on others. Or, maybe the problem really is that we don't feel worthy of all that care and attention; we don't deserve it. Then, too, it may just be that we are embarrassed by such attention and decide to suffer in isolation instead. (Each of these, or other, analyses should be imaged briefly in turn.)

3. Clues to resolution: The problem is, from James' point of view, all of these reasons leave the community deprived, first of its ministry of prayer and, second, of the connection to the member who is suffering. Because of the individualism at work in our communities, precisely when persons are most in need of each other, there is this tendency to close each other out. And if the ministry of prayer and healing cannot be shared with the sick, then it is difficult, too, to join in that "cheerfulness" as health returns. Instead, even as the member recovers, the community is left unhealed. So if we really are concerned about the health and healing of the church, we will need to listen to James more carefully. Neither suffering nor healing are solely individual matters; they affect the Body along with our bodies.

4. Experiencing the gospel: So what would it look like in our congregation if we heeded James? How would our life together be different? There would be frequent opportunities to share with each other our sufferings and struggles—in small groups and in the worshiping community on the Lord's Day. And certainly the prayer life of the community would be deepened. And, just maybe, more of that "cheerful" celebration would abound as well. (Here, the preacher will need to illustrate this interactive dynamic of need and prayer, perhaps with reference to how the community recently "did it right.")

5. Anticipating the consequences: Perhaps this is the time in the sermon to shift point of view. Take the perspective of those out in the church's parish who are not connected to any community of faith. They often suffer alone. What if such a person heard about the midweek service of prayer and healing at the church? How would they feel, coming into the building, receiving hospitality? And what kind of healing could already be celebrated that this person is now surrounded by a church family—forgiveness, reconciliation, salvation? We might want now to conclude the sermon with a celebration of this restoration and healing.

Mark 9:38-50. Once more, Mark presents the reversal of roles within the kingdom as involving a radical shift in the point of view of those who follow Jesus. The disciples report to Jesus that they attempted to forbid a charismatic healer "because he was not following us." Jesus' response shifts the framing of the healer's ministry from that of "following us" to serving "in my name." The effect is to locate the healer alongside the Twelve rather than in a position subordinate to them. Then, the issue is radically expanded, no longer focusing on just one itinerant healer; "Whoever is not against us is for us," Jesus announces. Then comes an even more drastic shift in point of view as Jesus locates the disciples among "these little ones" who should receive hospitality in the name of Christ. The "demotion" of the disciples is now complete. Instead of their deciding who is in and who is out, they are placed among the little ones whose sole claim to be "in" is the grace and hospitality of those who bear the name of Christ. A sermon on this text may want to invite the congregation to travel along the Way with its shifts in point of view. A series of moves or scenes in the sermon could then be plotted as follows:

1. "You are not one of us," cry the disciples! They forbid those who do not follow them.

Always the same cry with the same logic and the same conclusion. "Not following us leads to being forbidden, refused welcome. Today we hear the cry from liberals and evangelicals looking across the "great chasm" within our churches. Each side rebukes the other for "not following us." The conclusion is inevitable—the other side is not welcome. ("Following us" may be imaged with reference to theological positions or the approved list of social issues espoused by each side. Let the pastoral context decide.)

2. "No," Jesus insists, "Do not stop them." "If not against us, they are for us."

"Not against us, then for us" is the new rule. But what would that mean for us? It is really unsettling, not to have a "them" over against which we can define ourselves. Jesus would not allow the rich young man to define himself before God in opposition to the penitent sinner. Now, it looks like Jesus is talking to us, too! Just imagine who would be sitting next to us in church just now if this "welcome mat" were put out for those who are not against us. (A series of images here will be needed to give flesh to this striking idea.)

3. "Think of yourselves as 'children,' as 'little ones' in faith." You come with nothing that has earned you a place in God's family.

Now comes the most troubling shift. Think of yourselves as "little ones," as children or those brand new to faith. It means we take off all our "merit badges" of churchly service and join with those just come through the waters of baptism. There, those little ones know, it is all grace. Undeserving, they know they have been given new life, not earned it. (A recent baptism in the parish may well be the example of this move.)

4. "But blessed are those who welcome you, give you drink and do not make you stumble," Jesus proclaims.

So look, maybe we haven't been "demoted" after all. Didn't Jesus bless all the little children and welcome them? And now, he announces, we are to be welcomed too. But it looks like our days of "forbidding" anybody on the basis of whether they are "following us" are gone. Maybe it is enough to be welcomed ourselves. And what a wonderful thing it would be it those who are "in" welcome rather than forbid us. That would be, well, like the kingdom of God! (We need a strong illustration or image set here. How shall the congregation see and hear the gospel from this new point of view? There are some theological constraints to the illustrative system, though. We cannot now offer an individualistic story or example; the move is profoundly communal. And the point of view within the illustration or imagery will need to be consistent with that of the move itself. We are welcomed as little ones, and not those who are once more deciding who is in and who is out.)